home cooking WITH trisha yearwood

home cooking WITH
trisha yearwood

stories & recipes to share with family & friends

with **Gwen Yearwood & Beth Yearwood Bernard**
foreword by **Garth Brooks**

Clarkson Potter/Publishers
New York

Copyright © 2010 by Trisha Yearwood
Photographs copyright © 2010 by Ben Fink

Published in the United States by Clarkson Potter/Publishers, an imprint of the Crown Publishing Group,
a division of Random House, Inc., New York.
www.crownpublishing.com
www.clarksonpotter.com

CLARKSON POTTER is a trademark and POTTER with colophon is a registered trademark of Random House, Inc.

Originally published in hardcover in the United States by Crown Publishers, an imprint of the Crown Publishing
Group, a division of Random House, Inc., New York, in 2010.

All photographs are by Ben Fink with the exception of those appearing on the front cover (by Russ Harrington);
pages 8 and 202 (by Bev Parker); pages 50, 97 (bottom right), 136, and 224 (by Hope Baldwin). Photos appearing on
pages 56 (bottom left), 75, 78, 97 (bottom left), 108, 109, 163, 169, 176, 184, 194, and 208 are from the author's collection.

Library of Congress Cataloging-in-Publication Data is available.

ISBN 978-0-8041-3942-7
eISBN 978-0-307-98497-5

Printed in China

Book and cover design by Jennifer K. Beal Davis
Cover photograph by Russ Harrington

10 9 8 7 6 5
First Paperback Edition

dedication

There are those we've lost along the way who continue to live on in the sharing of these recipes and the telling of these stories. I can almost hear Garth's mom, Colleen, whispering in my ear, "The secret's the cinnamon!" when I'm making her cabbage rolls. Every time I make chocolate pie, I will see Ben Tillman smiling at me when I walk into the Tillman House and ask for fried chicken. I'll smile knowing that Miss Betty got to sign a few autographs along the way because of the success of her recipes in the first cookbook. And always, there is my daddy, humbly "apologizing" for some of the best meals I ever tasted, yet I know he feels proud seeing the people he loves the most represented in these pages. This book is dedicated to all those we love who aren't with us anymore but whose lives, stories, laughter, and good food are represented here.

We love you, always.
–Gwen, Beth, and Patricia

contents

foreword 9

introduction 11

helpful hints 14

breakfast 17

snacks and appetizers 39

soups and salads 59

beef and pork 81

chicken and fish 99

sides 113

breads 139

cakes and pies 155

cookies, candy, etc. 189

thanks 215
index 219

foreword

The greatest thing that can happen to an artist is to have someone come up to you and tell you how one of your songs has changed his or her life for the better. As an artist, you enjoy this experience so much. There is nothing in music that could please you more . . . until you see it happen to your spouse. Talk about pride! To see people's faces light up as they are telling Trisha how a song moved them to become more than what they were, to take chances, to take responsibility . . . to take control. That is what communicating and communicating well is all about. Now take that one step further. I cannot count the times I have seen someone approach Trisha with his or her cookbook in hand to either share a story or ask a question —and they always ask Trisha for her signature inside the cover. I have watched her tirelessly sign, exchange recipe tips, laugh, and swap stories over the first cookbook. If you have ever met Miss Yearwood and talked to her about family traditions and meals, then you will understand what I am about to say. I can't tell which one she enjoys more: cooking or singing! She does both with a love unequaled. As her husband, I am very proud of all of her accomplishments, and I am very happy for her success. But I find myself being even happier for her because she loves what she does. And I think that is the secret to her success in music and in cooking. The greatest compliment you can give a cook is to ask for more, and that is all I hear as I stand by and listen to people talk to Trisha. For those people and for myself, I am very happy to introduce a second helping of heartfelt recipes from our family to yours.

Garth Brooks

introduction

Never in my wildest dreams did I think I'd be sitting here writing an introduction to a second cookbook! Mom, Beth, and I were so overwhelmed and thrilled at the response to *Georgia Cooking in an Oklahoma Kitchen*. What a sweet surprise! We enjoyed getting to meet so many of you out on the road, and exchanging recipes and stories. I was happy to find out that our way of life was shared by many of you in all parts of the country, not just the south! What I learned from you was that you liked our family stories because they reminded you of your own lives, and that you liked our recipes because they were easy to prepare and didn't have a lot of fancy, hard-to-find ingredients. We decided to stick to the saying "If it ain't broke, don't fix it!"

We have a wonderful extended family, full of cousins, aunts, uncles, and friends who were kind enough to contribute recipes. For instance, it was from those family members and friends that we found my grandmother Elizabeth Yearwood's infamous Coconut Cake with Coconut Lemon Glaze recipe, which she used to make for my daddy.

Since we've received a lot of recipes that are traditions in our extended family but are new to us, we've been doing a lot of testing. We didn't want to include anything in this book that we hadn't made ourselves and didn't absolutely *love*. This has worked out well for our family members and friends, who have really benefited from our testing—and gained a few pounds to boot!

Some of these newer recipes already feel like old favorites. I make things like Crockpot Macaroni and Cheese, Baked Bean Casserole, and Asparagus Bundles so often now that they feel like dishes I've been making all my life. The Key Lime Cake recipe that I got from family friend Angela Spivey has become the new dessert hit at my house.

One of the best things about putting together this collection has been discovering new recipes. We all tend to stick to what we know, and I'm usually a bit wary about trying out something new on my family, but this cookbook has made me brave! It's a real treat for me to get to introduce some "new" old recipes to my family, like my grandma Lizzie Paulk's Old-Fashioned Strawberry Shortcake, and fresh ideas for breakfast, such as Apple Dumplings and Country Quiche.

I have always associated really good food with really good company. If you're with people you love, and you're having fun and loving life, great food is almost like another guest at the table. You laugh, talk, and savor a good appetizer together. Or you assign your friends the job of chopping up the vegetables while you fire up the grill. It's really all about being together, and enjoying life surrounded by people you love and food you can share!

Anyone can cook at home, but that doesn't necessarily make it home cooking. There's a lot of love in these pages that comes from generations of Yearwoods, Paulks, Bernards, Brooks, and beyond. *That's* home cooking. I'm proud to share this collection of recipes and stories with you.

helpful hints

- If you have a slow cooker, now commonly referred to as a crockpot, that is over ten years old, chances are it has a liner that isn't removable. Think about buying a new crockpot with a removable liner for easy cleanup. The liner is also great if you want to remove the pot to serve at the table.

- Never put hot water in a cold glass or ceramic pot or pitcher. If you're making tea, be sure to put some cold water into your cold pitcher before adding hot steeped tea. The same goes for cold to hot. Never put a hot ceramic or glass bowl into the sink and fill it with cold water. You can easily crack a nice pan or pitcher (or your new removable crockpot liner) this way. Let the pot cool completely before rinsing.

- Take the time to grate your own cheese instead of buying preshredded for use in a recipe. The agents sometimes used to keep commercially grated cheese from clumping give the cheese a waxy taste and a rough texture. Always read the label to look for additives to cheese.

- Cake Release made by Wilton is a product I've discovered that you can use instead of cooking spray or greasing and flouring your pans. It works great in all pans, but is especially good in Bundt pans and helps the cakes to release easily.
- When icing a cake, use a decorating turntable for easy turning. Cake-decorating turntables are fairly inexpensive (some under $10) and can be easily found at craft stores or online.
- Invest in an inexpensive offset spatula for frosting cakes and cookies. The slight bend makes icing a breeze.
- When baking a pie in a disposable metal pie plate, cut away the pan's outer rim with scissors to release the pie. This makes it much easier to cut slices of pie, and eliminates digging in the pan to get all the crust.
- Beater Blade makes a blade for stand mixers that has a rubber scraper on it. It basically works like a spatula and keeps your mixing bowl scraped while it turns. It works best in smooth cake batters.

breakfast

The saying is that breakfast is the most important meal of the day. People who think they aren't breakfast eaters should take a look at these dishes before they say no. Whether you like something light or hearty, sweet or salty, something that feeds a crowd or just one, there's a dish here for you. Breakfast was always a weekend treat for my sister and me as we grew up. Daddy didn't have to get up early and be at work on the weekends, so he would usually make us a huge breakfast that included bacon, sausage, eggs, grits, and homemade biscuits.

I'm a big believer that cooking for someone else is an act of love. We serve breakfast in bed to our moms on Mother's Day, our dads on Father's Day, or as a special treat for a birthday or anniversary, but you don't have to wait for a special occasion to show people you love them. Make every day special with these satisfying dishes.

mama's homemade waffles
with hot maple syrup

Pancakes and waffles were special morning treats at our house. As you might imagine, breakfast in a home where both parents worked and the children were running off to school every day was more often than not a quick piece of peanut butter toast or a bagel. We usually saved the big breakfasts for the weekends, and I remember waking up on Saturday mornings to the smell of something homemade cooking. Pancakes were a sweet breakfast surprise. Even today when I make them, I feel like it's a special occasion! We usually use one of our favorite store-bought syrups, but this Hot Maple Syrup from our cousin, SuSan Yearwood, is easy to make and also tastes great over Blueberry Pancakes (page 22). Just make sure to watch the syrup carefully once it starts to boil, reducing the heat as necessary to prevent it from boiling over. **MAKES 6 WAFFLES**

WAFFLES

2 cups sifted all-purpose flour

3 teaspoons baking powder

½ teaspoon salt

2 large eggs, separated

1½ cups milk

3 tablespoons unsalted butter, melted

Hot Maple Syrup (recipe follows)

Sift together the flour, baking powder, and salt.

Beat the egg whites until stiff. Set aside.

Beat the egg yolks. Add the milk and butter. Add the flour mixture, stirring until just blended. Fold in the beaten egg whites. Bake in a hot waffle maker that has been sprayed with cooking spray for about 5 minutes, until golden brown. Serve immediately with Hot Maple Syrup (page 20), melted butter, honey, or jam.

> FROM GWEN: This batter works great in a Belgian waffle maker, too.

> FROM BETH: Folding in the beaten whites makes these waffles really crisp.

hot maple syrup MAKES 4 CUPS

3 cups granulated sugar

2 cups light brown sugar

2 tablespoons dark corn syrup

2 cups water

2 teaspoons maple flavoring

2 teaspoons vanilla extract

1 teaspoon almond extract

Mix the sugars, syrup, water, maple flavoring, and extracts in a medium saucepan and cook over medium-high heat until the sugars dissolve. Bring the mixture to a boil, then reduce the heat to medium and simmer for 10 minutes, stirring occasionally, as the syrup reaches the correct consistency. Serve warm over pancakes or waffles. Store any leftover syrup in the refrigerator for up to 2 weeks.

Change it up by making bacon waffles. Cut bacon to fit each waffle grid. Close the cover and bake for 1 minute before adding waffle batter. Scramble some eggs and you have a complete breakfast.

blueberry pancakes

Like me, my nephew Kyle loves anything made with blueberries, and he also loves breakfast for supper, a tradition we have perfected here in Oklahoma. There really isn't any rule about when breakfast should be served. If we feel like having eggs and bacon for supper, we do it! Serve these pancakes topped with Hot Maple Syrup (page 20). SERVES 4 TO 6

1¾ cups all-purpose flour

2 tablespoons sugar

1 teaspoon baking powder

½ teaspoon baking soda

½ teaspoon salt

2 large eggs

1 cup milk

1 cup sour cream

¼ cup (½ stick) butter, melted

½ teaspoon vanilla extract

½ teaspoon lemon zest

1½ cups fresh or frozen blueberries

Sift the flour, sugar, baking powder, baking soda, and salt into a large mixing bowl. In a separate large bowl, lightly whisk the eggs. Add the milk, sour cream, melted butter, and vanilla, whisking to blend. Make a well in the dry ingredients and pour the egg mixture into it. Whisk the ingredients together just until blended. Fold the lemon zest and blueberries into the batter.

Heat a large skillet over medium heat or use an electric skillet on a medium setting. Use cooking spray or pour in vegetable oil to lightly coat the surface of the skillet. For each pancake, pour about ¼ cup of the batter into the hot skillet. Cook 3 or 4 pancakes at a time, depending on the size of the skillet. If the batter seems too thick, thin it with a little milk (1 to 2 tablespoons). When bubbles begin to form and "pop" on the pancake's surface (about 1 minute) and the outer edge looks done, flip it over and cook briefly (about 30 seconds) on the other side.

garth's breakfast bowl

Garth likes to cook breakfast. It's wonderful to sleep in and wake up to the smell of bacon cooking. Don't be too jealous, but he always has a fresh pot of coffee already made, too! He created this breakfast bowl because he wanted something really hearty. He's the first person I ever met who puts pasta with eggs and bacon, but it works, and it tastes great! If you're really hungry, all the better if you're going to eat one of these breakfast bowls. Don't worry if you can't finish it; Garth will come along later and "clean up"! **SERVES 4**

2 tablespoons butter

8 large eggs

1 16-ounce bag frozen hash browns or Tater Tots, thawed

1 pound pork sausage

1 pound bacon

1 9-ounce package cheese and roasted garlic tortellini

10 ounces sharp Cheddar cheese, grated (about 2½ cups)

In a large skillet, melt the butter and scramble the eggs.

In a separate large skillet, cook the hash browns according to package directions. In a third large skillet, break up the sausage with a wooden spoon and cook until browned. Drain off the excess fat. Transfer the sausage to a bowl. Cook the bacon in the same skillet. Drain on paper towels and set aside. Cook the tortellini according to the package directions. Layer a large bowl with hash browns, sausage, bacon, tortellini, eggs, and cheese.

Any potato will do. Garth's even been known to use french fries! I sometimes fry an egg sunny side up and pile it on top of Garth's bowl. He likes the way the yolk oozes into the dish.

country quiche

The first time I had quiche was in a quaint little café in Nashville. I loved it, and thought it was really fancy. You know how they say, "Real men don't eat quiche." Well, I don't even know who "they" are, but I'll bet you any real man would eat this quiche. It's full of all things good and very hearty. I turned Garth loose on this recipe and he suggested the tortellini. It made it even better. SERVES 16

1 pound ground pork sausage with sage

6 large eggs

1 teaspoon baking powder

20 grape tomatoes, sliced in half

10 ounces sharp Cheddar cheese, grated (about 2½ cups)

Salt and pepper

2 9-inch unbaked frozen pie shells

Preheat the oven to 350°F.

In a large skillet, cook the sausage until done, then drain off the excess fat and set aside.

Whisk the eggs, baking powder, and tomatoes together. Add the cooked sausage and the cheese to the egg mixture and stir together with a large spoon. Add salt and pepper to taste. Divide the mixture in half and pour into the unbaked pie shells. Bake for 30 minutes, or until the filling is set.

FROM GARTH: I boil some cheese tortellini and add it into the quiche before baking.

Set the frozen pie shells out to thaw a bit while you're preparing the quiche.

hawaiian fresh fruit salad

My family was lucky enough to go to Hawaii a few years ago for vacation. It was an incredible experience. Mama and I would wake up every morning looking forward to breakfast because the fruit was just amazing. I would eat fruit for breakfast every day if it tasted like those Hawaiian pineapples. Our cousin Lydia lives in Hawaii and gave us this recipe. She's lucky to be able to choose a variety of fresh fruit year-round. **SERVES 6**

6 cups of your favorite fresh fruits, such as:

Bananas, peeled and sliced

Blueberries

Pineapple, cut into bite-size pieces

Blackberries

Raspberries

Mango, peeled and cubed

Strawberries, stems removed and berries cut into halves

Kiwi, peeled, sliced, and each slice cut in half

Oranges, peeled and cut into chunks

⅓ cup fresh lime juice

1½ tablespoons honey

¾ teaspoon ground ginger or minced fresh ginger

Mix the fruit in a large salad bowl. Mix the lime juice, honey, and ginger in a small bowl. Pour the dressing over the fruit, and stir. Serve immediately if you use bananas. (If you make the salad ahead of time, hold out the bananas until just before serving.)

Watermelon is my favorite fruit, so I add chunks of it to this salad when it's in season.

apple dumplings

Quick and delicious! This is like having your own individual apple pie. My nephew Bret loves these served warm for breakfast. SERVES 8

2 Granny Smith apples
1 cup water
1 cup sugar
½ cup (1 stick) butter
¼ teaspoon vanilla extract
8 canned buttermilk biscuits
4 teaspoons ground cinnamon

Preheat the oven to 375°F.

Peel, core, and slice the apples vertically into 8 slices each. Cover with water to keep the slices from turning brown.

In a medium saucepan, mix the water, ¾ cup of the sugar, the butter, and the vanilla. Bring the sugar mixture to a boil over medium heat.

Separate each biscuit into 2 layers. Wrap a biscuit layer around a slice of apple, stretching the biscuit slightly to overlap, and seal on the bottom. Place the wrapped slices, sealed side down, in a 9 × 12 × 2-inch casserole dish. Pour the hot sugar mixture over the apple slices. Mix the remaining ¼ cup sugar with the cinnamon and sprinkle the mixture over the tops of the wrapped apples. Bake for 35 minutes, or until golden brown.

monkey bread muffins

Monkey bread is usually baked in a large tube pan and served by pulling off a "lump" of bread at a time. My niece Ashley tried this idea for making monkey bread in individual servings by downsizing the biscuit pieces and using our Hot Maple Syrup (page 20) in the mix. The muffins are a lot cuter and less messy! **SERVES 12**

1 12-ounce can biscuits (10 in each can)

3 tablespoons Hot Maple Syrup (page 20)

¼ cup (½ stick) butter, melted

⅔ cup sugar

1 tablespoon ground cinnamon

½ cup finely chopped pecans

NOTE: To make traditional monkey bread, grease all surfaces of a 10-inch tube pan. Drop the coated biscuit pieces evenly inside the tube pan. Pour the maple butter over the biscuits and bake at 350°F for 40 to 45 minutes. Let the bread stand for 5 minutes before turning out onto a cake plate. Pull off one lump at a time.

Preheat the oven to 375°F.

Place cupcake liners in 12 muffin cups. With kitchen shears, cut each biscuit into 4 pieces. In a small bowl, combine the maple syrup and melted butter. In a separate bowl, mix the sugar, cinnamon, and chopped pecans. Dip each biscuit piece into the maple butter, and roll in the sugar mixture. Place 3 or 4 coated pieces in each muffin cup, pressing to compact (see Note). Bake the muffins for 15 to 17 minutes. Allow to cool in the pan for 5 minutes before removing to wire racks. Serve warm.

cinnamon rolls

My daddy used to make the most amazing cinnamon rolls. I always think of him when I smell them baking. This recipe comes from a friend of Beth's. The neighborhood kids would know to go to Vicki's house at the first sign of snow because her mom would have a fresh batch of cinnamon rolls for them. We only get a little snow here in Oklahoma every year, and Mama and Beth *never* get snow, so we officially decided that any day, rain or shine, is a good day for homemade cinnamon rolls!   MAKES 2 DOZEN ROLLS

½ ounce (2 packages) active dry yeast

1 cup lukewarm (80–90°F) water

1 cup vegetable shortening, such as Crisco

¾ cup granulated sugar

1 cup boiling water

2 large eggs

6 cups self-rising flour

1 teaspoon salt

½ cup cinnamon sugar

1 cup (2 sticks) butter

2 teaspoons milk

1 16-ounce box confectioners' sugar

FROM GWEN: Make your own cinnamon sugar by mixing 2 teaspoons of ground cinnamon with ½ cup granulated sugar.

Butter the bottoms of four 9-inch round pans.

In a small bowl, dissolve the yeast in the lukewarm water. In a separate bowl, add the vegetable shortening and sugar to the boiling water. Set this mixture aside to cool slightly. In a large mixing bowl, beat the eggs and mix with the flour and salt. Add the dissolved yeast and the vegetable shortening–sugar mixture to the flour mixture. Mix until thoroughly combined. Cover the dough in the bowl with a clean towel and let it rise for 2 hours.

On a lightly floured surface, roll out the dough to a 19 × 14-inch rectangle and sprinkle with some of the cinnamon sugar. Slice 1 stick of butter into small pieces and dot all over the cinnamon sugar. Roll up the dough like a jellyroll and cut into 1-inch slices, using a heavy cotton thread or floss. Place the rolls in the prepared pans, cover, and allow them to rise for 2 hours.

Near the end of the rising time, preheat the oven to 350°F. While the oven preheats, melt the remaining stick of butter and add the milk and confectioners' sugar, mixing until smooth. Bake the rolls for 13 to 15 minutes, or until very light brown. Drizzle the icing over the rolls while they're hot.

beignets

I always say that I am not really a "sweets" person. The truth is I am more of a sweets snob. I like desserts, but only if they're homemade. One of my weaknesses, though, is doughnuts. I could live at Krispy Kreme and be happy. They give you a little hat to wear, they let you watch the doughnuts coming off the line, they smother them with glaze, and then they give you one, right off the assembly line. I immediately buy at least a dozen. These beignets are a little taste of Krispy Kreme heaven at home. All you need is a small baker's hat! **MAKES 5 DOZEN BEIGNETS**

¼ ounce (1 package) active dry yeast

1½ cups warm water (105°F)

½ cup granulated sugar

1 teaspoon salt

2 large eggs

1 cup evaporated milk

7 cups all-purpose flour, sifted

¼ cup vegetable shortening, such as Crisco

8 cups peanut oil

Confectioners' sugar for sprinkling

In the bowl of an electric mixer, sprinkle the yeast over the warm water. Stir to dissolve. Add the sugar, salt, eggs, and milk. Beat until blended. Add 4 cups of the flour by big spoonfuls. Beat until smooth. Add the shortening, and then beat in the remaining 3 cups flour. Cover the bowl with plastic wrap and chill in the refrigerator for 3 hours.

In a large electric fryer, preheat the oil to 360°F.

On a lightly floured surface, roll out the dough to a ⅛-inch thickness. Cut the dough into 2½-inch squares. Deep-fry each square in the hot oil for 2 to 3 minutes, or until lightly browned on each side. Drain on paper towels. Sprinkle heavily with confectioners' sugar.

FROM GWEN: Deep-fry in batches of about 12 at a time.

FROM BETH: Depending on the size of your electric fryer, it may take more or less than 8 cups of oil. Just pour the oil as deep as you can into your fryer.

snacks and appetizers

As I recall, we didn't do a lot of snacking in my family when I was growing up. Breakfast was either something on the fly or a big weekend bonanza. Lunch was from the school lunchroom. The lunch ladies at Piedmont Academy, where I went to school from first through twelfth grades, were amazing cooks, so lunch was always worth waiting for. Most children today aren't that jazzed about eating in their school cafeterias, but we had it made. Even the hamburgers were handmade right there in the school kitchen!

As an adult, I find myself making more dips and appetizers, sometimes in place of a meal. We have our friends and their children over on most weekends, and of course for special occasions like the World Series or the Super Bowl. Sometimes I'll make an entrée or Garth will grill steaks, and we'll ask them to bring sides—but more often than not, I'll say, "Let's just have snacks for everybody!" These snacks and appetizers are some of our must-haves.

corn salsa

I love fresh vegetables—especially in the summer. We always had a garden at home, and there just isn't anything quite like a homegrown tomato. This recipe pairs corn with garden-fresh tomatoes, jalapeño peppers, and cilantro. The resulting salsa is mouth-wateringly good and very easy to make. I serve it at summer birthday parties and on Super Bowl Sunday. SERVES 20

1 15-ounce can yellow corn, drained

1 15-ounce can white corn, drained

1 4-ounce can chopped green chiles, drained

1 2½-ounce can sliced black olives, drained

4 green onions, minced

2 medium tomatoes, finely chopped

2 jalapeño peppers, seeded and chopped

3 tablespoons white vinegar

⅓ cup olive oil

½ teaspoon salt

1 tablespoon finely chopped fresh cilantro

Tortilla chips, for dipping

Mix the corn, chiles, olives, onions, tomatoes, jalapeños, vinegar, oil, and salt in a medium bowl and chill in the refrigerator for at least 1 hour. Just before serving, add the cilantro. Serve with your favorite tortilla chips.

Substitute Fritos Scoops for plain tortilla chips. More salsa per bite!

watermelon salsa

Who says you need tomatoes to make salsa? Phyllis Pritchett of Martin, Tennessee, shared this recipe for a delicious summer salsa made with watermelon! This seemingly odd mix of ingredients makes an amazing appetizer. Add any fruit you like. I add diced mango sometimes for color and flavor. MAKES 3 CUPS

1½ teaspoons lime zest (from about 1 lime)

¼ cup fresh lime juice (from about 3 limes)

1 tablespoon sugar

¾ teaspoon pepper

3 cups seeded and finely chopped watermelon

1 cucumber, peeled, seeded, and diced

1 jalapeño pepper, seeded and minced

1 small red onion, finely chopped

8 fresh basil leaves, finely chopped

½ teaspoon garlic salt

Tortilla or pita chips

Stir together the lime zest, lime juice, sugar, and pepper. Add the watermelon, cucumber, jalapeño, onion, and basil and toss gently. Chill the salsa until ready to serve and add the garlic salt just before serving. Serve with tortilla chips or pita chips.

I like it spicy, so I use 2 jalapeños instead of 1!

charleston cheese dip

Cheese seems to be a staple in many southern dishes. I was on tour a few years ago and had a show in Charleston. When I got to my hotel room, the staff had left me a lovely basket of goodies. Usually, amenities baskets are full of things like fruit and candy. This basket was accompanied by a tray of homemade cheese dip and crackers. It was perfect for this Georgia gal! **SERVES 10**

½ cup mayonnaise

1 8-ounce package cream cheese, softened

1 cup grated sharp Cheddar cheese (about 4 ounces)

½ cup grated Monterey Jack cheese (about 2 ounces)

2 green onions, finely chopped

Dash of cayenne pepper

8 Ritz or butter crackers, crushed

8 slices bacon, cooked and crumbled

Preheat the oven to 350°F.

In a medium bowl, mix the mayonnaise, cream cheese, Cheddar cheese, Monterey Jack cheese, green onions, and cayenne pepper. Transfer the mixture to a shallow baking dish, such as a 9-inch pie pan. Top the mixture with the cracker crumbs and bake for 15 minutes, or until heated through. Remove the pan from the oven and top with the bacon. Serve immediately with corn chips, crackers, or bagel chips.

hot corn dip

I made this dip recently for "Girls' Night In." Every now and then a group of my girl-friends and I get together and watch our favorite television show, or watch chick flicks—insert your favorite movie here. My favorite tearjerker chick flicks are *Steel Magnolias, Return to Me,* and *Message in a Bottle.* We keep this dip warming in a slow cooker and snack on it all evening. Corn chips make this dip divine! SERVES 12

2 11-ounce cans Mexican corn, drained

2 4½-ounce cans chopped green chiles, drained

2 cups grated Monterey Jack cheese (about 8 ounces)

¾ cup grated Parmesan cheese

1 cup mayonnaise

Corn chips, for dipping

Preheat the oven to 350°F. Grease a 9 × 13 × 2-inch casserole dish.

In a medium bowl, mix the corn, chiles, cheeses, and mayonnaise until fully combined. Spread the mixture in the prepared casserole dish and bake, uncovered, for 30 to 40 minutes, or until bubbly around the edges. Serve the dip warm from the oven with corn chips.

spicy edamame dip

When I was a young girl, we had a big garden every year. I didn't know how good I had it until I moved to the big city of Nashville and ate my first canned vegetable! Aside from our personal garden, my daddy planted a big field each year with soybeans, which he sold at harvest. I never really understood why we grew something we didn't eat. I ended up loving soybeans. If I had known about this tasty dip back then, I doubt my daddy would have had many soybeans to sell! SERVES 12

4 large garlic cloves, unpeeled

16 ounces shelled edamame beans (about 2 cups)

1 teaspoon salt

½ teaspoon cayenne pepper

¼ teaspoon ground cumin

4 tablespoons olive oil

¼ cup fresh lime juice

¼ cup finely chopped fresh cilantro

Pita chips, for dipping

In a medium skillet over medium heat, roast the garlic, turning frequently, until softened, about 15 minutes. Remove from the heat, cool, and then slip off the skins. Set aside.

Bring about 8 cups of water to a boil in a saucepan and drop in the beans. Bring back to a boil and cook for 5 minutes. Reserve ¾ cup of the cooking water before draining. Drain the beans and cool.

Transfer the garlic into a blender and chop coarsely. Add the beans, salt, cayenne pepper, and cumin. Process in the blender, adding the reserved water a little at a time until smooth. (You may not need to add all of the water.) Add the olive oil, lime juice, and cilantro. Pulse to combine. Use pita chips for dipping.

cheese boat

This appetizer was shared with us by a South Georgia pastor's wife, Vicki Martin. She got it from a church hostess in Hawkinsville, Georgia, years before. The bread "boat" is a cute way to serve this warm cheesy appetizer. SERVES 10

1 loaf French or Italian bread

10 ounces sharp Cheddar cheese, grated (about 2½ cups)

3 2-ounce packages corned beef, such as Carl Buddig, finely chopped

½ bell pepper, cored, seeded, and finely chopped

½ teaspoon hot sauce, such as Tabasco

½ teaspoon chili powder

2 8-ounce packages cream cheese, room temperature

1 medium tomato, finely chopped

1 bunch green onions, finely chopped

Large corn chips

Preheat the oven to 350°F.

Cut an oval in the top of the loaf of bread, scooping out the bread in the center and making a "bread boat." Place the bread on a cookie sheet.

In a large bowl, mix the cheese, beef, bell pepper, hot sauce, chili powder, cream cheese, tomato, and green onions until fully combined. Spoon the mixture into the hollow center of the bread loaf. Bake for 30 minutes, until bubbling, and serve warm with corn chips.

jalapeño bites

My mom loves spicy dishes, and this recipe for a jalapeño pepper snack is one of her favorites. I've had deep-fried Cheddar jalapeño poppers at restaurants, but these cheesy bites use cream cheese and Parmesan for a different flavor. I really can't be left alone with these! **MAKES 36 BITES**

1 8-ounce package cream cheese, softened

8 ounces Parmesan cheese, grated (about 2 cups)

4 tablespoons seeded and chopped jalapeño peppers

1 large egg, beaten

3 cups dry plain bread crumbs

Preheat the oven to 350°F.

Mix the cream cheese, Parmesan cheese, jalapeños, and egg to form a paste. Shape into balls using about ½ tablespoon of paste for each. Roll the balls in the bread crumbs. Place on an ungreased baking sheet and bake for 10 to 15 minutes, until golden brown. Serve warm.

Handle hot chiles like jalapeño, habanero, or cayenne with care. Always wash your hands after handling. They may cause chemical burns to sensitive skin. If you've ever handled a hot chile and then scratched your eyes, you know what I'm talking about!

warren's chicken bites

My cousin Warren brought these little tidbits to a family reunion. He's a hunter and used dove breasts in his recipe. I'm embarrassed to say that I don't care for dove or quail. I'm even more embarrassed to tell you that after a big bird hunt, Mama would fry up everything Daddy brought home and I would eat Vienna sausages! I use chicken here, but I'm thinking ... Warren's Vienna bites! Hmmm ...   MAKES 8 BITE-SIZE SERVINGS

4 chicken tenders, flattened and cut in half

1 3-ounce package cream cheese, softened

2 teaspoons seeded and finely chopped jalapeño pepper

8 bacon slices

Top each piece of chicken with ½ teaspoon cream cheese and ¼ teaspoon jalapeño. Roll up each filling-covered chicken piece and wrap with 1 slice of bacon, securing with a toothpick. Grill for 8 to 10 minutes on an indoor grill. Or, if you are using an outdoor grill, turn the pieces once during grilling.

FROM GWEN: Substitute dove breast, dark meat chicken, or turkey for the chicken tenders, if you like.

Warren brought these bites, made with dove breast, to the Paulk family reunion.

georgia pâté

We love hummus, but couldn't think of a way for our recipe to be in a southern cookbook. Then we decided to replace the standard garbanzo beans with boiled peanuts, one of our favorite snacks, and voila!—redneck hummus.   MAKES 2 CUPS

1 15-ounce can or 2 cups fresh shelled boiled peanuts (see Note)

5 tablespoons tahini (see second Note)

2 teaspoons lemon zest

3 tablespoons fresh lemon juice (about 1 lemon)

2 tablespoons chopped fresh parsley

2 teaspoons minced garlic

¼ teaspoon cayenne pepper

2 tablespoons olive oil

6 tablespoons water

Using a food processor, blend the peanuts, tahini, lemon zest and juice, parsley, garlic, and cayenne pepper until coarsely chopped. With the processor running, pour the olive oil through the top opening in a slow, steady stream, processing until the mixture is smooth. Remove the mixture to a mixing bowl and stir in the water for desired spreading consistency. Serve with your choice of chips, crackers, or vegetables.

NOTE: Boil your own fresh green peanuts in a 3-quart stockpot, covering them with water and adding ⅔ cup salt for each gallon of water used. Bring to a boil, then reduce the heat to medium and cook for 1½ hours, or until the nuts are tender. Drain and cool.

NOTE: Tahini isn't always easy to find. Make your own by blending ¼ cup vegetable oil with 1 cup toasted sesame seeds. Store the extra in the refrigerator for up to 2 weeks.

FROM GWEN: This is delicious on strips of sweet red bell pepper.

six-week pickles

Louise Aiken, a ninety-four-year-old family friend, has her own garden and grows her own cucumbers. She gave Mama three jars of these pickles at Christmas, one for each of us. They went fast! Louise was given the recipe by a Monticello, Georgia, friend, Nona Wilson. The time spent on these pickles is mostly just waiting. **MAKES 6 PINTS**

6 pounds cucumbers (about 16 medium), 1½ inches in diameter

2 quarts white vinegar

4 pounds sugar

4 scant drops cinnamon oil

4 scant drops clove oil

FROM GWEN: Louise buys cinnamon oil and clove oil at the local drugstore. Since the recipe calls for only a few drops, the tiny bottles last forever and she just shares hers with me.

Wash the cucumbers thoroughly. Pack the whole cucumbers in a 1-gallon widemouthed glass jar. Do not trim the ends of the cucumbers. Fill the jar with enough vinegar to cover the cucumbers. Cover and set aside at room temperature for 6 weeks.

After 6 weeks, drain the cucumbers in a colander. Do not rinse the cucumbers. Trim the cucumber ends and slice into ⅛- to ¼-inch slices.

Put a layer of cucumber slices back into the glass jar and layer with the sugar. Repeat the layering process until you've used all of the cucumber slices and sugar. Add the cinnamon and clove oil. The jar will be about three-fourths full. Shake the jar at least four times during the day or stir with a wooden spoon to distribute the sugar and oils. The vinegar on the cucumbers will dissolve the sugar. Set aside for 2 or 3 days to allow the sugar to dissolve and the oil flavors to develop. Transfer the pickles to pint jars for storage.

Most pickle recipes include endless soaking in lime and rinsing. This one is super-easy.

sweet tea

This was the first thing I remember making at home as a child. Sweet tea is the staple of every good southern meal. I like it warm, right after it's made, but most people love it cold and over ice. I had been making this tea for many years before I realized I was making it wrong. My sister was watching me make it one day and said, "Whoa! You're putting way too much sugar in that!" I guess the original Yearwood recipe calls for ¾ cup sugar. Too late to turn back now! This really should be called Sweet Sweet Tea. MAKES 1 GALLON

4 large, family-size tea bags
16 cups water
1½ cups sugar

Fill a teakettle or saucepan with enough water to completely cover the tea bags, about 2 cups. Bring to a boil and remove from the heat. Let the tea stand for 10 minutes. Put the sugar into a gallon pitcher and add 1 cup of cold water. Stir to mix slightly. Pour the hot tea into the sugar mixture and stir until the sugar is dissolved. Stir in the remaining 13 cups of cold water to fill the pitcher.

If using a glass pitcher, mix the sugar with 1 cup cold water before adding the hot tea to prevent the pitcher from cracking.

red candy apples

You have to be pretty confident in your dental work to eat these! Beth lost her first tooth while eating a candy apple. What a sweet treat for the tooth fairy! Candy apples always remind me of Halloween carnivals, so we usually come home after trick-or-treating (yes, I still dress up!) and make these with our friends and all of the children. I'm not sure who eats more, the kids or the adults. **MAKES 8 CANDY APPLES**

Chopped peanuts or pecans

8 firm apples, such as Jonathan or Fuji

8 popsicle sticks

2 cups sugar

½ cup water

1 cup light corn syrup

1 2-ounce box Red Hots cinnamon candy

Few drops of red food coloring

> FROM GWEN: Substitute 1 drop of cinnamon oil or peppermint oil for the Red Hots candy.

Bring a medium pot of water to a boil. Grease a cookie sheet with cooking spray. Set aside.

Put the chopped nuts in a shallow bowl. Set aside. Wash the apples thoroughly. Remove the stems from the apples and insert a stick into the center of the bottom of each apple. To remove any wax that may coat the apples, dip each apple quickly in the boiling water. Drain and dry the apple.

In a medium saucepan, bring the sugar, ½ cup water, and syrup to a boil. Cook to 250°F, or until the syrup spins a thread when poured from the edge of a cooking spoon. Pour in the candy pieces and continue cooking to 285°F. Remove from the heat and add the food coloring to achieve the desired shade of red.

Dip the apples quickly in the hot mixture, twisting as you dip to cover the entire apple. Roll the apples in the nuts, coating the bottom half of each apple. Place on the greased cookie sheet and allow the coating to cool and harden. (The syrup can be reheated if it cools too much during the dipping process.)

Opposite, left: Mc and Beth, Halloween 1967. Mama made our costumes!

soups and salads

When I think about ordering soup and a salad at a restaurant, I am usually in the mood for a light lunch or dinner. There are some great summer salads in this chapter, but there are also hearty soups, chilis, and salads that will really fill you up! Many things here can be served as meals right by themselves.

I usually crave soup on a cold or rainy day, but I am guilty of making soup in late summer, before it's quite cold enough, because I just can't wait until the first chilly day!

The salads are great starters, wonderful entrées, and perfect accompaniments to a sandwich.

chicken soup

We had never heard of Gold Medal Wondra flour before seeing
this amazing soup, and we figured we'd never find it in our local grocery stores. But Beth
found it on the shelf at Harvey's grocery store in Tifton, Georgia! It is a very fine flour that
dissolves quickly so you don't end up with lumps in your gravy or soup. It's pretty
awesome. Who knew? This recipe comes from our cousin Donna Paulk, who started
making this soup when her very young grandsons didn't like baby food. **SERVES 10**

Salt and pepper

4 whole chicken breasts,
bone in and with skin

2 medium bell peppers, cored,
seeded, and chopped

2 medium onions, chopped

1 cup chopped celery

1 48-ounce can chicken broth

3 medium red potatoes,
chopped

1 16-ounce package frozen
mixed vegetables

1 cup tricolor rotini pasta,
uncooked

1 cup small carrots, cut
lengthwise into fourths

3 tablespoons Wondra or
all-purpose flour

2 cups (16 ounces) heavy
whipping cream

¼ cup (½ stick) butter

Sprinkle salt and pepper on each chicken breast and place in an
8- to 10-quart stockpot. Add the bell peppers, onions, and celery,
then pour the chicken broth over all. Bring to a boil. Reduce the
heat to a simmer and cook the chicken for 40 to 50 minutes, or
until done.

Transfer the chicken to a bowl. Allow to cool slightly. Remove the
bones and skin and discard. Shred the chicken and put back into
the pot. Add the potatoes and cook for 12 to 15 minutes. Add the
mixed vegetables and cook for 12 to 15 minutes more. Add the
pasta and carrots, and cook for 7 minutes more. In a quart glass
measuring cup, mix the flour into ¼ cup water until smooth.
Pour in the cream, then add to the soup mixture along with the
butter. Cook for 10 more minutes. Allow to stand for at least
15 minutes before serving.

FROM BETH: If you can't
find this magic flour at your
local grocer, use all-purpose
flour and make sure to whisk
out any lumps. Of course,
you can always take a road
trip to Tifton, the Turfgrass
capital of the South!

rainy day chicken and rice soup

Everybody craves soup on cold, wintry days. I love this rainy-day soup, even in the summer. Most soups have rice, potatoes, or pasta, but rarely all three. Maybe we should nickname this "exercise" soup since it's loaded with carbohydrates. I like to have a big bowl of this over cornbread, then take a nap, but that's just me. SERVES 8

4 boneless, skinless chicken breast halves

5 chicken bouillon cubes

1 small onion, finely chopped

2 tablespoons dried parsley

½ teaspoon pepper

8 cups water

6 carrots, peeled and sliced

4 medium potatoes, peeled and cubed

6 ounces fettuccine noodles

1 12-ounce brick American cheese, cubed (about 3 cups)

¾ cup instant rice, uncooked

In a large stockpot, boil the chicken, bouillon cubes, onion, parsley, and pepper in the water until fully cooked, about 30 minutes. Remove the chicken from the broth and strain the broth into a large bowl. Discard the onion mixture. Allow the chicken to cool. Cut into cubes.

Measure the broth and add enough water to make 8 cups of liquid in the large stockpot. Bring the broth to a boil. Add the carrots and potatoes, and cook for 20 minutes, or until the potatoes are done. Add the noodles and cook for 10 minutes more. Remove the pot from the heat and add the cheese and rice. Stir the mixture and let it stand for 10 minutes before serving.

tennessee jambalaya

This hearty kielbasa sausage stew comes from Beth's Tennessee pal Colleen Cates. Cajun jambalaya recipes call for any meat that walks, crawls, swims, or flies! We decided this dish is the Tennessee version of Louisiana jambalaya, sans seafood! Serve over rice.

SERVES 6

4 slices bacon

1 to 1½ pounds kielbasa sausage, thinly sliced

1½ teaspoons onion powder

2 15.5-ounce cans black beans with juice

2 8-ounce cans tomato sauce

1 4-ounce can green chiles

2 medium carrots, shredded

½ teaspoon Italian seasoning

⅛ teaspoon pepper

In a large stockpot, cook the bacon until crisp and set aside. Cook the sausage in the bacon drippings until lightly browned. Stir in the onion powder, black beans, tomato sauce, chiles, carrots, and seasonings. Bring the stew to a boil, then reduce the heat and simmer, covered, for 45 minutes. Stir occasionally. Crumble the bacon and sprinkle on top of the stew before serving. Serve over rice.

fancy chili

Everybody has his or her own favorite chili recipe. I've never had one that I could really call mine until now. I make this nonstop during the winter. It not only tastes great but is also pretty in the bowl, with the colorful peppers and carrots. That's why I call it Fancy Chili. This chili is awesome served over Sour Cream Cornbread (page 144). SERVES 4

1 tablespoon olive oil

2 garlic cloves, minced

½ cup chopped green onion

½ pound lean ground beef

2 tablespoons hot chili powder

1 28-ounce can fire-roasted diced tomatoes

1 15-ounce can black beans, rinsed and drained

1 medium bell pepper, cored, seeded, and diced

4 carrots, peeled and grated

½ teaspoon brown sugar

Pinch of salt

In a large saucepan, heat the oil over medium heat. Add the garlic and green onion, and cook for about 1 minute. Add the ground beef and cook until browned, about 5 minutes. Stir in the chili powder until fully combined. Add the tomatoes, beans, bell pepper, carrots, brown sugar, and salt. Bring the mixture to a boil, then reduce the heat to low. Cover and simmer the chili for 15 minutes.

FROM BETH: This chili is really good with ground turkey breast substituted for the ground beef.

Save some of the green onion for a garnish, if you like. I serve my chili over rice with a dollop of sour cream. What's a dollop, anyway?

lettuce wedge with blue cheese dressing

I was an adult before I acquired a taste for blue cheese, but I love the strong flavor of it, and nothing beats homemade salad dressing. This creamy dressing served over the lettuce wedge is simple, yet satisfying. SERVES 8

Juice of 1 large lemon

1 cup mayonnaise

1 cup buttermilk

½ cup sour cream

1½ teaspoons garlic powder

1½ teaspoons onion powder

6 ounces blue cheese, crumbled (about 1½ cups)

2 heads iceberg lettuce

10 slices bacon, cooked and crumbled

1 medium tomato, finely diced

In a medium mixing bowl, combine the lemon juice, mayonnaise, buttermilk, sour cream, garlic powder, and onion powder. Whisk the mixture together until smooth. Add the cheese and mix just until blended. Chill in an airtight container in the refrigerator for at least 2 hours before serving (makes 2½ cups).

Core and quarter each head of lettuce and divide among 4 salad plates.

Serve a generous dollop over each lettuce wedge and top with bacon and tomato.

Leftover dressing can be stored in an airtight container in the refrigerator for up to 2 weeks.

strawberry salad

In late February or early March, it's strawberry time in Georgia. We look for every opportunity to put a strawberry in something—from appetizers to desserts. Fresh sliced strawberries in this cool garden salad have made it a favorite at our house. What a tasty way to get your fruit and veggies! **SERVES 4 TO 6**

1 package ramen noodles, crushed, flavor packet discarded

¼ cup sunflower seeds

¼ cup sliced almonds

¼ cup (½ stick) butter, melted

1 head romaine lettuce, washed and dried

1 5-ounce bag baby spinach

1 pint strawberries, hulled and thinly sliced

1 cup grated Parmesan cheese

¾ cup sugar

½ cup red wine vinegar

2 garlic cloves, minced

½ teaspoon salt

½ teaspoon paprika

¾ cup vegetable oil

Preheat the oven to 350°F.

In a small bowl, mix the ramen noodles, sunflower seeds, almonds, and melted butter. Transfer to a baking sheet and toast in the oven, stirring occasionally, until browned, about 10 minutes. Remove from the oven and set aside to cool.

Tear the lettuce and combine with the spinach, strawberries, and Parmesan cheese in a large salad bowl.

Dissolve the sugar in the vinegar. Combine the garlic, salt, paprika, and oil, and then add to the sugar-vinegar mixture. Mix well and store in the refrigerator until ready to serve.

Just before serving, sprinkle the crunchy topping over the salad greens and toss the salad with enough dressing to coat the greens.

> FROM BETH: To save time, this salad can be made *without* the crunchy topping. It will still be delicious.

cornbread salad with french dressing

Cornbread served at every meal is a southern thing. I was surprised the first time I traveled west of the Mississippi to find out that not everybody serves cornbread with every meal! Here, putting the bread in the salad makes it really hearty. Add the homemade dressing, and you don't need anything else, except maybe a glass of Sweet Tea (page 54)!
SERVES 6

SALAD

6 cups torn romaine lettuce pieces

2 cups crumbled Sour Cream Cornbread (page 144)

4 medium tomatoes, chopped

1 small green bell pepper, finely chopped

1 medium sweet onion, such as Vidalia, finely chopped

French Dressing (recipe below)

9 slices bacon, cooked and crumbled

Layer the ingredients in a large salad bowl, beginning with the lettuce, then adding the cornbread, tomatoes, bell pepper, and onion. Let stand in the refrigerator for 3 hours.

When ready to serve, pour the dressing over the salad and sprinkle the bacon on top.

french dressing   MAKES 3 CUPS

½ cup apple cider vinegar

½ cup water

1 cup sugar

1 teaspoon salt

1 tablespoon paprika

1 tablespoon grated onion

1 tablespoon yellow mustard

1 cup vegetable oil

Put the vinegar, water, sugar, salt, paprika, onion, mustard, and oil in a blender and process until well blended. Chill in the refrigerator.

ty's thai salad

I had this salad at California Pizza Kitchen when I was in Los Angeles with Garth for a series of concerts he did to benefit the victims of the southern California wildfires in 2008. I loved this salad so much that I decided to try to re-create it at home. I still order their salad every time I'm in Los Angeles, and I think this one comes pretty close to the original! SERVES 12

1 head napa cabbage, shredded

1 head red cabbage, shredded

2 boneless, skinless chicken breasts, cooked, chilled, and thinly sliced

1 large cucumber, julienned

1 10-ounce bag shelled edamame, cooked

2 carrots, peeled and grated

4 green onions, finely diced

Sweet Lime-Cilantro Dressing (recipe below)

1 avocado, peeled and finely sliced

In a large serving bowl, toss the cabbages, chicken, cucumber, edamame, carrots, and green onions. Top each serving with 2 tablespoons of Sweet Lime-Cilantro dressing and 2 slices of avocado, for garnish.

Just before serving, I add crispy wontons, a few dry-roasted peanuts, and a dash of peanut sauce.

sweet lime-cilantro dressing   MAKES 2 CUPS

2 cups olive oil

Juice of 2 limes

2 garlic cloves, minced

1½ cups finely chopped fresh cilantro

1 cup sugar

½ teaspoon salt

½ teaspoon pepper

Put the oil, lime juice, garlic, cilantro, sugar, salt, and pepper in a large blender and blend until smooth.

marinated vegetable salad

The salad is usually the last thing you prepare before serving a meal, so you're working on it when you may feel rushed to get the food on the table. This colorful salad is prepared ahead and marinated overnight so it's ready to serve when you are. **SERVES 8 TO 10**

1 cup red wine vinegar

1 cup sugar

½ cup olive oil

1 teaspoon salt

16 ounces frozen or fresh shelled green peas, cooked 3 minutes and drained

16 ounces cut green beans, frozen or fresh, cooked 3 minutes and drained

2 small sweet onions, thinly sliced

1 2-ounce jar chopped pimiento

1 red bell pepper, cored, seeded, and chopped

1½ cups thinly chopped celery

Bring the vinegar and sugar to a boil in a medium saucepan. Add the oil and salt and set aside to cool. Add the peas, beans, onions, pimiento, bell pepper, and celery. Transfer the mixture to a bowl, cover with plastic wrap, and marinate in the refrigerator for 24 hours. Drain and serve.

FROM GWEN: You may substitute canned peas and beans.

uncle marshall's ham salad

My uncle Marshall was a truck driver. He drove a big blue Peterbilt truck and kept his cigarettes rolled up in his shirtsleeve. I thought he was the coolest guy on the planet. I never dreamed he could cook! He's gone now, but his granddaughter, Christy, used to watch him make this salad, and she shared his recipe with me. When I make the salad, I still picture him outside working on his truck. Real men cook! SERVES 6

3 cups ground or finely diced fully cooked ham (about 14 ounces)

1 teaspoon finely chopped sweet Vidalia onion

2 teaspoons sweet pickle relish

½ cup mayonnaise

1 tablespoon yellow mustard

Combine the ham, onion, relish, mayonnaise, and mustard. Serve on crackers or in a sandwich.

Grandaddy Paulk standing beside Uncle Marshall's Peterbilt truck, 1974.

My uncle Marshall Edward Paulk was a truck driver.

chicken poppy seed salad

Everybody loves the basic, tried-and-true chicken salad recipe that I make, but I had this chunky chicken salad at the Paulk family reunion in Willacoochee, Georgia, this past spring and I fell in love with it. The recipe comes from Lindsey Rundorff, who is the great-granddaughter of my great-aunt Cora Paulk, my mama's aunt. Draw that one on your family tree! Aunt Cora was all of four feet eleven inches tall, one of the sweetest ladies you could ever know, and a real pistol. She lived to be ninety-six years old. She'd be tickled pink to know she ended up in a cookbook! **SERVES 12**

2½ pounds boneless, skinless chicken breasts

4 celery stalks, finely chopped

4 cups seedless grapes, halved

2 cups slivered almonds

2 cups mayonnaise

¼ teaspoon salt

¼ teaspoon pepper

2 tablespoons poppy seeds

2 tablespoons dried dill

Boil the chicken in a large pot filled with water until done, about 45 minutes. Drain the chicken and set aside to cool. Once the chicken is cooled, dice into small pieces and place in a large mixing bowl. Add the celery, grapes, almonds, mayonnaise, salt, pepper, poppy seeds, and dill. Mix until the salad is fully combined. Store in the refrigerator.

I add mandarin oranges if I have them in the pantry, just for fun.

shamrock salad

This is a favorite of my mom's. Grandma Yearwood served this at the first meal my mom had with the Yearwood family after she met my dad. Daddy was an only child, so it must have been pretty intimidating to sit with just Mrs. Elizabeth and Mr. Bo for dinner! The fact that my mom is a really good cook, too, was an icebreaker for them, and I think it was the first thing they liked about her–besides the fact that Daddy was obviously crazy about her! SERVES 10

1 3-ounce package lime-flavored gelatin

1 cup boiling water

$\frac{2}{3}$ cup evaporated milk

1 9-ounce can crushed pineapple with juice

1 tablespoon fresh lemon juice

1 12-ounce container cottage cheese

$\frac{1}{2}$ cup finely chopped celery

$\frac{1}{2}$ cup mayonnaise

$\frac{1}{2}$ cup finely chopped pecans

10 lettuce leaves

10 lime slices, for garnish

In a medium bowl, stir the gelatin into the boiling water. When the gelatin is completely dissolved, stir in the evaporated milk, pineapple, lemon juice, cottage cheese, celery, mayonnaise, and pecans. Pour the mixture into a 1½-quart square clear glass dish. Chill overnight, or until firm. Cut the chilled salad into squares and serve on lettuce leaves. Garnish with twisted lime slices.

Elizabeth Winslett Yearwood, 1950s.

beef and pork

I am a meat-and-potatoes girl! I adhere to the
latest recommendations that say we *should* eat lean red meat,
just not every day of the week. I think that's all the more
reason to make sure that when you do eat red meat, it's something special. You can choose lean meats for all of these
recipes and they will still taste rich and hearty!

I grew up loving pork. You can definitely tell in this collection of recipes that I love bacon! I tend to avoid ribs because
they're usually so hard to eat, but my cousin Fred's Barbecued
Pork Ribs (page 97) are fall-off-the-bone good.

uncle wilson's stuffed b

My uncle Wilson is just one of those people. You know, the
and a kind word for you. I have so many memories of him
smiling, and cooking great food. He made his debut in our
Onion Association even put him on their Web site. I'm not sure if he's too famous now to
take my calls, but I'm sure glad he's still sharing recipes, like this one, with me. These
peppers are one of his specialties. I do love his cooking, almost as much as I love him!

SERVES 6

6 large red or green bell peppers

2½ cups long-grain white rice (or rice of your choice)

2 pounds lean ground beef

½ medium-size sweet onion, such as Vidalia, diced

2 garlic cloves, finely chopped

1 14.5-ounce can diced tomatoes, with their juices

1 10-ounce can Rotel diced tomatoes and green chilies

16 ounces sharp Cheddar cheese, grated (about 4 cups)

½ teaspoon pepper

1 teaspoon salt

Preheat the oven to 400°F.

Cut the bell peppers in half, top to bottom. Remove the seeds
and the ribs. Set aside. In a medium saucepan, cook the rice
according to package directions. In a medium skillet, brown the
ground beef, onion, and garlic. Drain the meat. In a medium
saucepan, bring the tomatoes to a boil, then reduce the heat and
simmer for 5 minutes. Remove from the heat. In a large bowl,
combine the ground beef, rice, tomatoes, pepper, and salt and
mix until blended.

In a 9 × 13 × 2-inch pan, place the bell peppers skin side down.
Evenly divide the beef mixture among the pepper halves. Cover
the pan with aluminum foil and bake for 40 minutes. Remove
the foil and sprinkle the cheese on the top. Return the pan to the
oven, uncovered, for about 5 minutes, until the cheese melts.

FROM GWEN: Before using,
wilt the pepper halves in
boiling water for about
5 minutes. This will reduce
the cooking time from
40 minutes to 15.

*A Fourth of July "must-have" at the
annual gathering of family and friends.
The secret? Aunt Beth helps him!*

[Col]leen's cabbage rolls

My mother always told me it's a no-win situation to try to cook things for your husband "just like his mama used to make." I agree with her, but I also believe taste is a strong sense that can evoke wonderful memories. This dish was among Garth's family's favorites made by his mother, Colleen. I doubt that my version, taken from her handwritten recipe, is as good as hers, but I think it makes Garth smile and remember his mom when I make it. Colleen always said the secret to this dish was the cinnamon! SERVES 6

½ pound lean ground beef

1 cup long-grain white rice, cooked

½ teaspoon salt

¼ teaspoon pepper

¼ teaspoon ground cinnamon

¼ teaspoon ground cloves

1 8-ounce can stewed tomatoes

2 heads green cabbage

9 cups water

2 tablespoons sugar

1 tablespoon lemon juice

1 tablespoon vinegar

2 bay leaves

1 12-ounce can tomato juice

Preheat the oven to 350°F.

In a large bowl, mix the beef, rice, salt, pepper, cinnamon, cloves, and tomatoes. Set aside.

Wash and core the cabbage. Bring a large stockpot filled with 8 cups of the water, the sugar, lemon juice, vinegar, and bay leaves to a boil. Blanch the cabbage in the boiling mixture for 5 minutes, or just until softened. Drain the cabbage, let it cool, then carefully peel 12 leaves from the cabbage.

Place ¼ cup of the beef and rice mixture onto each leaf. Fold in the sides of the leaf and wrap into a roll, enclosing all the filling. Place the cabbage rolls, seam side down, closely together in a 9 × 13 × 2-inch shallow baking pan.

In a small bowl, combine the tomato juice with the remaining 1 cup water and pour the mixture over the cabbage rolls. Cover the pan with aluminum foil and bake for 45 to 50 minutes, or until the meat is well done.

I use 2 heads of cabbage to get the 12 biggest leaves possible. If the outside of your cabbage has bright green leaves, discard them. They won't get as tender in cooking as the brighter leaves underneath.

baked spaghetti

This dish meets all the requirements for the perfect potluck take-along. It's a crowd pleaser, it's big enough to feed a crowd—and it's easy to transport. Beth takes this to church suppers, but I just make it for Garth and the girls. We never have any leftovers!

SERVES 12

6 slices bacon

1 teaspoon minced garlic

1 cup chopped onion

1 cup chopped bell pepper

3 14.5-ounce cans diced tomatoes with liquid

1 2.25-ounce can sliced ripe black olives, drained

1–2 tablespoons dried oregano, according to taste

1 pound ground beef, browned and drained

12 ounces thin spaghetti, cooked and drained

2 cups grated Cheddar cheese (5 ounces)

1 10-ounce can cream of mushroom soup

¼ cup water

¼ cup grated Parmesan cheese

Preheat the oven to 350°F. Grease a 9 × 13 × 2-inch baking dish.

In a large skillet, cook the bacon until slightly crisp, then cut it into smaller pieces. Remove the bacon and sauté the garlic, onion, and bell pepper in the bacon drippings until tender. Add the tomatoes, olives, oregano, bacon, and the cooked beef. Simmer this mixture, uncovered, for 10 minutes. Place half of the spaghetti in the prepared pan. Top the spaghetti with half of the vegetable-beef mixture. Sprinkle this layer with 1 cup of Cheddar cheese. Repeat the layers. Mix the canned soup and water until smooth, and pour over the casserole. Sprinkle the top with Parmesan cheese. Bake, uncovered, for 30 to 35 minutes, or until heated through.

FROM BETH: This entrée is also good if you substitute mozzarella cheese for the Cheddar.

cordelia's roast beef

Nothing smells better than a roast cooking in the oven—the Dutch oven, that is. This roast smells great all over the house as it slowly simmers in its own gravy. When my friend Mandy comes over for this meal, she loves the smell so much that she will go outside and come back in, just to get the full effect all over again! If there is any left over, use it to make hash (see recipe below). **SERVES 8**

2 tablespoons salt

1 3-pound eye of round beef roast

½ cup all-purpose flour

3 tablespoons vegetable oil

2 10-ounce cans French onion soup

1 10-ounce can golden mushroom soup

Rub the salt into the meat very well. Coat the meat with flour.

In a large cast-iron Dutch oven, heat the vegetable oil. Sear the roast on all sides. Transfer the seared roast to a platter and scrape the pan to loosen the drippings. Add the soups and 3 soup cans of water to the pan. Bring to a boil, then reduce the heat to a simmer, return the roast and its juices to the pan, cover, and cook for 3 hours, or until the meat is tender.

Slice and serve with the pan gravy.

roast beef hash MAKES 12 ½-CUP SERVINGS

2 cups roast beef drippings (cooking liquid)

4 tablespoons all-purpose flour

2 cups water

1 small onion, chopped

1 pound leftover beef roast, chopped or shredded

1 4-ounce can evaporated milk

Pour the drippings from cooking a roast into a measuring cup and let the fat rise to the surface. Skim off the fat, reserving 4 tablespoons in a saucepan and discarding the rest. (If the fat measures less than 4 tablespoons, add enough butter to make up the difference.) Measure the defatted pan juices; if you have less than 2 cups, add water to make 2 cups. Boil the pan juices, the 2 cups water, and the onion until the onion is clear. Add the beef and return to a boil. Remove from the heat and stir in the evaporated milk. Serve over rice, grits, or cornbread.

I also like the hash over buttered toast with eggs.

slow-cooker pork loin

Before I found this recipe, my attempts at cooking pork loin usually began with high hopes and ended with dry, overcooked meat. The secret is the slow-cooking crockpot. Spices in the rub get a chance to really flavor the loin, and it doesn't dry out. In fact, it's so tender that it actually falls apart! SERVES 8

1 2½- to 3-pound pork loin
½ teaspoon garlic powder
¼ teaspoon ground ginger
1/8 teaspoon dried thyme
¼ teaspoon black pepper
1 tablespoon cooking oil
2 cups chicken broth
2 tablespoons lemon juice
3 teaspoons soy sauce
3 tablespoons cornstarch
Salt and pepper

Trim the visible fat from the loin. If necessary, cut the roast to fit into a 3½-, 4-, or 5-quart crockpot. In a small bowl, combine the garlic powder, ginger, thyme, and pepper. Rub the spice mixture over the entire surface of the loin. In a large skillet, heat the oil and brown the loin slowly on all sides. Drain off the fat. Transfer the loin to the crockpot. Combine the chicken broth, lemon juice, and soy sauce; pour over the loin. Cover and cook on a low-heat setting for 8 to 10 hours or on a high-heat setting for 4 to 5 hours. When the roast is done, transfer the meat to a serving platter and cover to keep it warm. To make the gravy, pour the juices from the crockpot into a glass measuring cup. Skim off the fat. Measure 2 cups of liquid, adding water to the juices, if necessary, to make 2 cups. Transfer the juices to a saucepan, reserving ½ cup. Stir the cornstarch into the reserved ½ cup of juice until dissolved, then stir into the juices in the saucepan. Heat, stirring frequently, until the gravy is thickened and bubbly, 5 to 7 minutes. Cook and stir 2 minutes more. Season the gravy to taste with salt and pepper. Slice the roast and serve it with the gravy.

meatballs

In my busy life, I just don't have time to try complicated recipes. I think I always assumed homemade meatballs had to be really difficult and time-consuming. One day my friend Kim came over and showed me how to make these meatballs. They are so easy to make and so good! She likes to make the bigger ones, but I like the small bite-size ones. Simmer these meatballs in your favorite spaghetti sauce for 30 minutes.

MAKES 20 MEDIUM MEATBALLS OR 35 SMALL MEATBALLS; SERVES 10

2 pounds lean ground beef

½ pound ground pork

2 cups Italian-flavored bread crumbs

4 medium eggs, lightly beaten

1 cup milk

½ cup fresh parsley, finely chopped

2 garlic cloves, minced

1 medium onion, minced

Preheat the oven to 350°F.

In a large bowl or mixer, thoroughly mix the beef, pork, bread crumbs, eggs, milk, parsley, garlic, and onion. Chill in the refrigerator for 30 minutes. Shape into meatballs and place on a foil-lined shallow baking pan. Bake 30 minutes for medium- or 25 minutes for bite-size meatballs.

Stick toothpicks in these meatballs and serve them as an appetizer.

cowboy lasagne

In my introduction to *Georgia Cooking in an Oklahoma Kitchen*, I mentioned that Garth had recently asked me about trying to create a heartier, meatier lasagne, and we started experimenting. Here's what we came up with. Remember those old commercials that said, "How do you handle a hungry man?" Well, here's how! **SERVES 12**

1 pound lean ground beef, chuck or round

1 pound sage-flavored sausage

1 medium onion, finely chopped

1 garlic clove, minced

2 tablespoons olive oil

1 pound sliced pepperoni

1 16-ounce can tomatoes, diced or stewed

1 12-ounce can tomato paste

2 cups water

2 teaspoons salt

½ teaspoon pepper

1 tablespoon dried oregano

16 ounces lasagna noodles

16 ounces ricotta cheese

16 ounces mozzarella cheese, shredded

1 cup grated Parmesan cheese

Preheat the oven to 350°F.

In a large, heavy skillet, lightly brown the ground beef, sausage, onion, and garlic in the oil. Be sure to keep the meat chunky, not finely separated, while cooking. Drain the meat. Add the pepperoni, tomatoes, tomato paste, water, salt, pepper, and oregano. Simmer, uncovered, for 30 minutes.

Cook and drain the lasagna noodles according to package directions.

In a 9 × 13 × 2-inch baking pan, spread 1 cup of the prepared sauce. Alternate layers of lasagna, sauce, ricotta, mozzarella, and Parmesan cheeses, ending with sauce, mozzarella, and Parmesan. Bake for 40 minutes, or until lightly browned and bubbling. Allow the dish to stand for 15 minutes before serving. Cut the lasagne into 3-inch squares and serve.

> FROM BETH: My family likes cottage cheese in place of ricotta. It gives the lasagne even more texture.

Serves 12 regular people or 1 hungry cowboy and his wife!

pork medallions

The combination of ginger and orange makes this a tasty recipe. The little medallions, garnished with orange slices, are pretty, too. The tenderloin cooks quickly. The only thing you have to remember is that you need to marinate the pork the night before you want to serve it. SERVES 8

½ cup teriyaki marinade

¼ cup apple cider vinegar

2 tablespoons minced garlic

¼ cup ginger sauce

¼ cup orange juice

2 pork tenderloins, about 1 pound each

4 tablespoons olive oil

1 medium red onion, coarsely chopped

¼ cup teriyaki sauce

¼ cup V8 juice

¼ cup honey

¼ cup orange marmalade

2 oranges

Mix the teriyaki marinade, vinegar, garlic, ginger sauce, and orange juice. Pour this mixture over the tenderloins in a roasting pan. Cover and refrigerate overnight.

The next day, preheat the oven to 350°F.

Heat the olive oil in a heavy skillet. Remove the tenderloins from the marinade and put them, along with the chopped onion, in the hot oil. Sear the meat on all sides. Return the pork and onion to the marinade in the roasting pan. Cover loosely with foil and bake for 20 minutes.

Mix the teriyaki sauce, V8 juice, honey, and orange marmalade. When 20 minutes are up, remove the pork from the oven, remove the foil, and with a very sharp knife cut deep slits into the meat. Pour the honey sauce into these slits and over the meat. Slice the unpeeled oranges into ¼-inch crosswise pieces and arrange on the top and sides of the tenderloins. Return the meat to the oven and bake, uncovered, for an additional 15 minutes, or until the orange slices begin to curl. Remove the meat from the oven and let stand for 10 minutes before slicing into medallions. Transfer to a platter to serve.

fred's barbecued pork ribs

My cousin Fred was the organizer of the first Paulk reunion in Willacoochee, Georgia, in 1993. He said from the beginning, "Ya'll come and I'll provide the meat. You can bring something if you want to but it's more important that you come." He's kept his promise by providing delicious pork ribs every time. His "special spray" makes these ribs flavorful. We recommend that you have your butcher cut each pork rib slab in half lengthwise and then into two-rib sections. They cook faster and are easier to handle and eat.

SERVES 10 TO 15

6 pounds meaty pork rib slabs

4 tablespoons seasoned salt (with onion and garlic)

4 tablespoons lemon pepper seasoning

1 cup lemon juice

1 cup apple cider vinegar

2 tablespoons Worcestershire sauce

Preheat an electric or gas grill to 250°F.

Rub all sides of the pork with the seasoned salt and lemon pepper seasoning. Put the rib sections on the grill. Prepare Fred's Special Spray by mixing the lemon juice, vinegar, and Worcestershire sauce. Put this mixture in a food-safe spray bottle. Spray the ribs with Fred's Special Spray. Cook the ribs until they are browned, about 1½ hours, spraying often with the sauce. Put the ribs in a 4-inch deep stainless-steel pan with a lid. Spray the ribs once more and close the lid completely. Increase the grill temperature to 300°F and cook the covered ribs for 3 hours more.

For the second cooking, you can substitute a baking bag for the covered pan and cook the ribs in a 300°F oven for 3 hours.

Fred Paulk, 1957.

Fred Paulk playing the harmonica at the Paulk family reunion.

chicken and fish

I love chicken and am always looking for a new way to serve it. Garth loves anything in a casserole, so you'll find that many of the recipes in this chapter are a meal in a dish. All of the fish we ate growing up came from our own pond, so I don't have any fancy fish recipes.

And growing up in middle Georgia made it difficult to get fresh seafood, so we usually saved our shrimp and crab eating for beach vacations. We finally learned to make our own Low-Country Boil (page 110) and we enjoy that every summer.

chicken piccata

This dish is the result of a collaboration of two people who've never even met! Beth's neighbor Hope Kozma and Stone Workman, a friend in Monticello, Georgia, both make delicious chicken piccata, so we combined the best of theirs! If capers are not your thing, substitute frozen green peas for a tasty alternative. SERVES 4 TO 6

¼ cup olive oil

2 large eggs

½ cup all-purpose flour

½ cup grated Parmesan cheese

1 pound thinly sliced boneless, skinless chicken breasts

5 tablespoons butter

½ teaspoon minced garlic

1 cup chicken broth

1 3.5-ounce jar capers, rinsed and drained

1 tablespoon fresh lemon juice

1½ tablespoons white wine vinegar

2 tablespoons chopped fresh parsley

FROM BETH: If using regular boneless chicken breasts, flatten them with a meat mallet to uniform thickness.

Heat the olive oil on the stovetop in a large skillet over medium heat.

Beat the eggs in a shallow bowl. In a separate dish, mix the flour and Parmesan cheese. Dredge the chicken pieces in the eggs and then in the flour-cheese mixture.

Add 2 tablespoons of butter to the heated olive oil, and when the butter melts, add the floured chicken breasts. Cook for 3 to 4 minutes on each side, until browned. Transfer the chicken to a platter and set aside.

Add the remaining 3 tablespoons of butter and the garlic to the skillet drippings. Sauté the garlic for 30 seconds, being careful not to burn it. Add the chicken broth and capers to the skillet, stirring to mix. Cook the liquid for 3 to 5 minutes over medium-low heat, until reduced by half. Add the lemon juice and vinegar, and heat through. Return the chicken to the skillet, spooning some of the sauce over the chicken. Cover the skillet and cook for an additional 8 to 10 minutes over medium heat, until the sauce bubbles and the chicken is cooked through. Sprinkle with chopped parsley and serve.

If the sauce is too tangy to you, substitute ½ cup white wine for the vinegar to get a milder flavor.

chicken pizza

After discovering a delicious chicken pizza on a family beach trip, we decided to create it at home. We love this recipe because it's so different from traditional pizza—not a tomato in sight. Now we can all enjoy it more than once a year! SERVES 12 TO 14

2 13.8-ounce cans premade pizza crust dough

4 tablespoons olive oil

2 teaspoons minced garlic

2 cups shredded mozzarella cheese (about 8 ounces)

2 cups shredded Cheddar cheese (about 8 ounces)

1 bell pepper, cored, seeded, and cut into strips

1 red onion, sliced vertically

3 boneless, skinless chicken breast halves, grilled and diced

6 slices bacon, cooked until crisp and crumbled

Preheat the oven to 350°F.

Roll the pizza dough out and fit onto two 15-inch pizza pans. Drizzle 1 tablespoon of olive oil and 1 teaspoon of garlic on each pizza crust, followed by ½ cup each of the mozzarella cheese and ½ cup of the Cheddar cheese. Scatter half of the bell pepper, sliced onion, chicken, and bacon on top of the cheeses. Sprinkle another ½ cup mozzarella cheese and ½ cup Cheddar cheese over each pizza and drizzle each pizza with 1 tablespoon more of olive oil. Bake the pizzas for 20 to 25 minutes, or until the crusts are lightly browned. Slice each pizza into 8 pieces.

Pizza doesn't have to be round! I make this pizza dough into a rectangle and cut it into squares to serve.

linda's chicken and dressing

Our cousin Linda Paulk brought this chicken and dressing casserole to our family reunion, and I loved it. It combines all the things I love about my grandma Lizzie's cornbread dressing with the poultry all in one dish. Linda doesn't use a recipe, but she was kind enough to write one down for me! SERVES 12

1 hen, about 4 pounds (see Note)

Salt and pepper

1 8-inch pan prepared cornbread (about 1 pound)

32 saltine crackers, crumbled

10 slices white bread, torn into pieces

8 large eggs, boiled and chopped

2 tablespoons olive oil

1 medium onion, chopped

4 celery stalks, diced

NOTE: A hen is more flavorful, but if you can't find one, substitute a roasting chicken.

In a large pot with a lid, cover the hen with water and add 1 tablespoon salt and ½ teaspoon black pepper. Bring the water to a boil. Reduce the heat, cover, and simmer the hen until tender, about 1 hour and 30 minutes, or until the meat falls off the bone. Reserve the broth and meat separately and discard the bones.

In a very large bowl, crumble the cornbread, crackers, and bread crumbs. Add the chopped eggs. In a medium saucepan, heat the olive oil and cook the onion and celery until tender, about 7 minutes. Add ¼ cup of the reserved chicken broth and continue cooking until the vegetables are translucent, about 6 minutes. Add the onion and celery to the bread mixture. Add 2 cups of the broth and mix well using a sturdy spoon or your hands. Continue adding broth until the mixture is very moist, almost soupy. Put the dressing in a 9 × 13 × 2-inch casserole dish. Press chunks of boiled hen into the dressing, using about three fourths of the meat. Cover the casserole and refrigerate overnight.

The next day, preheat the oven to 350°F. Remove the casserole from the refrigerator and let stand at room temperature while the oven is heating. Bake for 45 minutes, or until heated through. The dressing should be moist. If it appears to dry out too much overnight, pour another cup of broth over it.

chicken spinach lasagne

The mention of spinach in a recipe usually sends a few folks running from the dinner table, but in this twist on lasagne, one taste will have them asking for more. Beth's friends often gather in each others' homes for a weekend bring-a-dish, and when it's her turn to host, she usually makes this lasagne. Even the kids like it! You can put it together ahead of time and bake it just before dinner is to be served. It's great with some wild rice and a green salad. The spinach can just be your little secret! **SERVES 12**

1 10-ounce package frozen spinach, thawed and drained

2 boneless, skinless chicken breast halves, cooked and shredded

2 cups grated Cheddar cheese (5 ounces)

1 small onion, finely chopped

1 tablespoon cornstarch

½ teaspoon salt

¼ teaspoon black pepper

1 tablespoon soy sauce

1 10-ounce can cream of mushroom soup

1 8-ounce container sour cream

½ cup sliced fresh mushrooms

⅓ cup mayonnaise

8 ounces lasagna noodles, cooked according to package directions

1 cup grated Parmesan cheese

1 cup pecans, finely chopped

Preheat the oven to 350°F.

In a large bowl, combine the spinach, chicken, Cheddar cheese, onion, cornstarch, salt, pepper, soy sauce, soup, sour cream, mushrooms, and mayonnaise. Put a layer of noodles in the bottom of a greased 9 × 13 × 2-inch casserole dish. Spread half of the spinach mixture over the noodles. Put another layer of noodles over the mixture and cover with the remaining spinach mixture. Sprinkle the Parmesan cheese over the casserole. Then sprinkle the pecans on top. Bake for 1 hour. Let the casserole sit for 15 minutes before serving.

chicken and wild rice casse

Including the fresh vegetables we grew in our summer garden, Beth an_____ _____ ʋn basic foods: meat, potatoes, white rice, and gravy. That pretty much cove_____ __ y meal you'd ever need. My mama was serving up the dishes that her mama, Lizzie, taught her to make. I think we were all slow to try new things, because we knew what we liked, and we didn't change things that much. This dish is the first "new" recipe I remember trying that had wild rice in it. I thought I was doing something crazy by eating wild rice! This dish has now become a regular at my dinner table. I love to take this casserole to parties or church suppers. **SERVES 10 TO 12**

2 4½-ounce cans sliced mushrooms, drained (reserve juice), or 16 ounces sliced fresh mushrooms

1 cup (2 sticks) butter

1 small onion, chopped

½ cup all-purpose flour

3 cups chicken broth

3 cups half-and-half

4 boneless, skinless chicken breast halves, cooked and diced

2 6-ounce boxes long-grain and wild rice mix, such as Uncle Ben's, cooked

1 cup slivered almonds, toasted and coarsely chopped

½ cup sliced pimiento

4 tablespoons chopped fresh parsley

1 teaspoon salt

½ teaspoon pepper

Preheat the oven to 350°F. Grease a 9 × 13 × 2-inch casserole dish.

If you use fresh mushrooms, sauté them in a large skillet with 1 tablespoon of butter until tender, about 10 minutes. Drain and reserve the juice.

In a large skillet, sauté the onion in the remaining butter until tender. Stir in the flour, cooking for 2 to 3 minutes. Combine the mushroom juice with enough broth to make 3 cups of liquid. Slowly stir the juice-broth mixture into the onion mixture. Stir in the half-and-half. Cook until the mixture is thickened. Add the sautéed or canned mushrooms, the chicken, rice, toasted almonds, pimiento, parsley, salt, and pepper. Pour into the prepared casserole dish. Bake, uncovered, for 30 to 45 minutes, until most of the liquid is absorbed.

saucy bass

My great-grandmother Mary Paulk had a large farm pond in Willacoochee, Georgia. She liked to paddle a boat out into the dark waters and fish for bream with a cane pole. My grandaddy Paulk fished for bass with a rod and reel, often taking my mom along to paddle for him. I'll bet they never cooked bass this way! **SERVES 4**

2 teaspoons salt

1½ pounds largemouth bass fillets (8 fillets total)

½ cup ketchup

½ cup mayonnaise

1 tablespoon yellow mustard

1 tablespoon Worcestershire sauce

¼ cup brown sugar

2 teaspoons apple cider vinegar

½ cup olive oil or salted butter, melted

½ cup chopped sweet onion

1 lemon, sliced

Preheat the oven to 300°F.

Line a 9 × 13 × 2-inch casserole dish with aluminum foil. Salt the bass and transfer it to the dish.

Make the basting sauce by mixing the ketchup, mayonnaise, mustard, Worcestershire sauce, brown sugar, vinegar, olive oil, and onion. Pour the sauce over the bass and bake for 40 to 45 minutes, or until the meat flakes easily with a fork. Spoon the sauce over the fish at 20-minute intervals as it bakes. Using pancake turners, carefully remove the fish to a platter and garnish with lemon slices.

Try substituting other fish, such as whole rainbow trout. Adjust the baking times by testing flakiness.

My daddy proudly displaying his largemouth bass!

Mary Paulk with her catch.

pete's catfish

My eighty-eight-year-old cousin Pete Yearwood is an experienced fisherman and catches large catfish. My daddy, Jack, was an only child, so his few remaining relatives are very special to me. Pete reminds me a lot of my daddy, from the sparkle in his eyes to his great sense of humor. When my dad built our house in 1970, he found a fresh spring down in the woods. He built a pond out of that spring, and he would often take Beth and me fishing. He baited our hooks for us and removed them from our catches long after we were old enough to do it ourselves. We never caught a fish as big as Pete's, though! SERVES 6

6 large catfish fillets

1 tablespoon plus 1 teaspoon salt

1 cup cornmeal

2 tablespoons all-purpose flour

¼ teaspoon black pepper

2 quarts peanut oil

Put the catfish in enough water to fully cover. Add a tablespoon of salt, cover with plastic wrap, and soak overnight in the refrigerator.

Mix the cornmeal, flour, 1 teaspoon salt, and black pepper in a plastic bag. Drain the water from the catfish and transfer the fish to the bag with the cornmeal. Shake the bag to coat the fish.

FROM GWEN: A steak from one of these fish is more than a serving. Pete says the key to a good piece of fish is in the way it's cut. He cuts 1-inch slices, crosswise, from the largest part of the fish, then fillets one side of the remaining tail portion and leaves the bone in the other side.

Heat the oil in a deep fryer or Dutch oven to 300°F. Drop a few pieces of fish into the hot oil. Do not overcrowd. Cook the fish until golden brown, about 10 minutes. Remove the pieces with a slotted spoon and keep warm in an oven while frying the remaining pieces.

FROM BETH: Serve this fish with a side of Jalapeño Hushpuppies (page 152).

Pete holding a 45-pound flathead catfish that he caught in 2008, when he was eighty-seven years old! He was fishing in the Oconee River near his home in Greensboro, Georgia, with a rod and reel. He had to have a little help holding this one!

low-country boil

The only thing I knew about Low-Country Boil before I tried it for myself was a scene from the movie *Steel Magnolias*, where Dolly Parton is serving it up at a county fair to Julia Roberts. (I should just say, Truvy is serving Shelby. All true Southerners know this movie by heart.) My family has always loved the beach, and this recipe makes me look forward to going. Of course, you don't have to have a beach to make it. The guys usually cook this outdoors over a gas flame, and by the time the crowd gathers, it's ready to eat. Don't expect any leftovers. **SERVES 15 TO 20**

1 8-ounce bottle concentrated Louisiana-style shrimp and crab boil seasoning, like Zatarain's Liquid

8 pounds medium red potatoes

5 medium sweet onions, such as Vidalia, peeled

5 pounds cured, smoked pork sausage links, cut into 3-inch pieces

16 8-inch ears of corn, cut in half

8 pounds raw medium shrimp

FROM BETH: Use whole potatoes. Cutting them before boiling will cause them to be mushy.

Fill a 10-gallon stockpot half full with water. Add the seasoning and bring to a rolling boil. Add the whole potatoes to the pot. Allow the water to return to a boil and cook for 5 minutes. Add the onions and sausage. Bring the water back to a boil and cook for 15 minutes. Add the corn, bring the water back to a boil, and cook for 10 minutes, or until the potatoes are done. Add the shrimp, bring the water back to a boil, and cook until the shrimp turn pink, about 3 minutes. Drain through a colander, discard the liquid, and serve on a large platter or on newspaper.

It is easier to cook a large Low-Country Boil over a gas cooker outside.

sides

Obviously, I love to cook for my family and my friends. At first, they would ask if they could bring a side for dinner, and I would say no. I didn't want anybody else to have to spend time in the kitchen when I was more than happy to make the entire meal, top to bottom. I learned, though, that it feels good to bring something to the table. It brings everyone closer together if each has had a hand in preparing the meal. Now, if people ask if they can bring a side dish or if they can help in the kitchen, I say, "Yes!"

For example, I think our girls enjoy the Asparagus Bundles (page 127) more if they have helped cut the spears and wrap the bacon themselves. They can be proud that they were a part of preparing the meal, and they are learning that most of these sides are very easy to make. I hope their participation will encourage them to cook more when they are grown and out on their own. In the meantime, I'll tell you what's for supper, and you can bring one of these delicious sides to go with it!

okra and tomatoes

If you only like okra fried, you may be surprised at this pretty combination dish. Choose small okra pods. They're the most tender. SERVES 6 TO 8

1 small onion, finely chopped

1 bell pepper, finely chopped

2 garlic cloves, minced

1 tablespoon butter

⅓ cup ketchup

½ cup grated carrot

1 teaspoon dried basil

2 large tomatoes, diced

1 10-ounce can tomatoes with chiles, such as Rotel brand

3 cups sliced fresh okra, in ½-inch pieces

In a medium skillet, sauté the onion, bell pepper, and garlic in the butter until tender. Add the ketchup, carrot, basil, and fresh and canned tomatoes, then cook 10 to 15 minutes more. Add the okra and continue cooking until the vegetables are tender, taking care not to overcook the okra. Serve over rice or as a side dish.

If you prefer a less spicy dish, dice 2 large, fresh tomatoes rather than the canned tomatoes with chiles.

crunchy slaw

My memories of meals in my hometown of Monticello, Georgia, involve a lot of Styrofoam containers—at chicken barbecues at horse shows, pork barbecue fund-raisers for the Boy Scouts, fish fries at our family friends the Hickeys' farm, and lots more. Daddy cooked a lot of chicken, pork, and stew in those days and slaw was a required side dish on those plates. It was always a mayonnaise-based slaw, so I thought that was the only kind in existence. By the way, I'm sure there's some law about having mayonnaise—and butter, for that matter—in every dish that comes out of the state of Georgia. If there isn't, there should be! My sister, Beth, recently shared with me this tasty slaw recipe with lots of crunch and a sweet-and-sour dressing. **SERVES 10 TO 12**

SALAD
1 head green cabbage, finely chopped

8 green onions, finely chopped

½ cup sliced almonds

½ cup sesame seeds

¼ cup (½ stick) butter

2 3-ounce packages ramen noodles, flavor packets discarded

DRESSING
2 tablespoons sugar

½ cup vegetable oil

3 tablespoons red wine vinegar

1 teaspoon salt

½ teaspoon pepper

Mix the cabbage and green onions in a large bowl. In a small saucepan over medium heat, brown the almonds and sesame seeds in the butter.

Combine the dressing ingredients in a small bowl and stir well. Just before serving, add the sesame seeds, almonds, and crushed raw ramen noodles to the cabbage and green onions. Pour the dressing, a little at a time, over the salad mix, then toss.

broccoli casserole

My mama was a schoolteacher for twenty-five years. She even taught me in the third grade! My best friend in elementary school was Julie Perry. Julie's mom taught the second grade, and Julie had already had her mom as a teacher, so she showed me the ropes. People always ask me if it was weird having my mama for a teacher and I always say yes. I never knew whether to call her "Miss Yearwood" or "Mama"! Julie and I were friends from the first grade all the way through high school graduation. We spent lots of time at each other's homes, working on school projects or having "spend the night" parties. I ate a lot of meals at Mr. Edwin and "Miss" Julianne's house. This recipe came from Mrs. Perry.

SERVES 8 TO 10

2 10-ounce packages frozen chopped broccoli, or 1 pound fresh broccoli florets

2 large eggs, beaten

1 cup mayonnaise

1 10-ounce can cream of mushroom soup

4 tablespoons grated sweet onion

10 ounces sharp Cheddar cheese, grated (about 2½ cups)

Salt and pepper

½ cup bread crumbs, crushed regular potato chips, or cheese cracker crumbs

Preheat the oven to 350°F. Butter a 9 × 13 × 2-inch casserole dish.

Cook the broccoli in water, drain, and set aside to cool.

In a large bowl, combine the broccoli, eggs, mayonnaise, soup, onion, and 2 cups of the grated cheese. Add salt and pepper and put into the prepared casserole dish. Bake for 30 minutes. Remove the casserole from the oven and sprinkle the surface with the cracker crumbs. Top with the remaining cheese. Return to the oven and bake until the crumbs brown slightly and the cheese melts, about 10 minutes.

squash casserole

My sister, Beth, was always the squash eater in our family. Just the thought of the yellow stringy stuff could send me from the table. This is the recipe that changed it all for me. I have Garth to thank because he loves squash casserole, so I went in search of a recipe. Beth shared this one with me (of course). I tasted it just to be nice, and never looked back. I am now officially a squash eater! **SERVES 8**

2 pounds yellow summer squash, trimmed and sliced ¼ inch thick

½ small sweet onion, such as Vidalia, peeled and diced

1 teaspoon salt

1 large egg

½ cup mayonnaise

½ cup grated Cheddar cheese (about 2 ounces)

¼ teaspoon black pepper

½ cup butter crackers, such as Ritz, crushed (about 12 crackers)

Preheat the oven to 350°F. Butter a 2-quart casserole dish.

Place the sliced squash and the onion in a medium saucepan with about a cup of water and ½ teaspoon of the salt. Cover and cook over medium until the squash is tender, about 15 minutes. Drain and cool.

Put the squash into a bowl and beat with an electric mixer; the mixture should remain kind of chunky. Add the egg, mayonnaise, cheese, remaining ½ teaspoon salt, and the pepper and mix until combined. Pour the squash mixture into the prepared dish, top with the crumbs, and bake for 30 minutes.

The natural moisture content of a squash varies with the variety and with growing conditions. Choose a yellow straight or crookneck summer squash, and drain the cooked squash thoroughly before combining it with the other ingredients.

crockpot macaroni and cheese

There are a lot of recipes in this book that I cook every week. This is a dish that I would make every day, but I rarely do because I simply can't be alone with it! I love macaroni and cheese, and this recipe is the bomb. After the time is up, and you open the crockpot lid for the first time to see the cheese and butter just bubbling on the top, you will fall in love. Be prepared to eat the entire dish—and don't say I didn't warn you! SERVES 12

8 ounces elbow macaroni, cooked

1 12-ounce can evaporated milk

1½ cups whole milk

2 large eggs, beaten

¼ cup (½ stick) butter, melted

1 teaspoon salt

Dash of pepper

2 10-ounce bricks sharp Cheddar cheese, grated (about 5 cups)

Dash of paprika

In a large 4-quart crockpot sprayed with cooking spray, mix the macaroni, milks, eggs, butter, salt, pepper, and all but ½ cup of the grated cheese. Sprinkle the reserved cheese over the top of the mixture and then sprinkle with paprika. Cook on low heat for 3 hours and 15 minutes. Turn off the crockpot, stir the mixture, and serve hot.

If you don't have a crockpot, grease a 9x13x2-inch pan with butter, add the mixture, and bake at 350°F for 50 minutes.

vegetable pie

A friend of mine brought this pie to lunch one day, saying that she had just thrown in some vegetables that she had on hand. That's the great thing about this dish—you can vary the ingredients based on what you like or what you have in your garden or refrigerator! I recently rediscovered the recipe when we had an overabundance of yellow squash and zucchini, and it quickly became a summer specialty in my family. **SERVES 12**

1 tablespoon olive oil

1 garlic clove, minced

1 cup peeled and chopped sweet onion, such as Vidalia

1 large zucchini squash, thinly sliced

1 large yellow squash, thinly sliced

½ teaspoon salt

½ teaspoon pepper

1 cup mayonnaise

1½ cups grated mozzarella cheese (about 6 ounces)

1½ cups grated Cheddar cheese (about 6 ounces)

2 large tomatoes, peeled and cut into ¼-inch slices

2 9-inch deep-dish pie shells, prebaked as directed

1 8-ounce can water chestnuts, drained

Preheat the oven to 325°F.

Heat the olive oil in a medium skillet over medium heat. When hot, add the garlic and sauté for 2 minutes; don't let it brown. Add the onion, zucchini squash, yellow squash, and half of the salt and pepper. Cook until the squash is tender, about 15 minutes. Divide the mixture in half.

Mix the mayonnaise and cheeses and set aside. Layer the sliced tomatoes in the bottom of the baked pie crusts. Sprinkle the tomatoes with the remaining salt and pepper. Layer the squash mixture on top of the tomatoes, then layer the water chestnuts. Top each pie with half of the mayonnaise and cheese mixture. Bake, uncovered, for 40 minutes. Allow the dish to stand for 15 minutes before cutting into wedges and serving.

asparagus bundles

I went through my entire childhood thinking I hated asparagus. I remember telling my mom I didn't like it, and I remember her asking, "Have you ever even tried it?" I can feel heads nodding right now. Of course I never tried it! It was green. I was a kid. Need I say more? I was over thirty years old before I finally tried asparagus. I'm making up for lost time now. I love it any way that it's prepared. These bundles make it look almost too pretty to eat. SERVES 6

2 pounds fresh asparagus, ends trimmed

12 slices bacon

½ cup light brown sugar

½ cup (1 stick) butter

1 tablespoon soy sauce

½ teaspoon garlic salt

¼ teaspoon freshly ground pepper

Preheat the oven to 400°F.

Divide the asparagus spears into 12 bundles. Carefully wrap 1 piece of bacon around each bundle, starting about ½ inch from the bottom of the tips. Secure the bacon-wrapped spears with a toothpick. Lay the bundles in a low-sided casserole dish.

In a medium saucepan, combine the brown sugar, butter, soy sauce, garlic salt, and pepper. Bring the mixture to a boil. Pour the hot sugar mixture over the asparagus bundles. Transfer the dish to the oven and roast for 25 minutes, or until the spears have begun to wilt and the bacon looks fully cooked. Remove the toothpicks before serving.

twice-baked potatoes

My mama used to make these for us when we were children. Potatoes fixed any way are my favorite vegetable, and this combines the idea of baked potatoes with mashed potatoes. You really can't go wrong. When I think about how I grew up, I feel very lucky. Our parents always ensured, even as our lives got busier, that we had time together as a family. Getting together every evening for supper was a way to share great food and talk about our day. **SERVES 12**

6 large baking potatoes

2 tablespoons olive oil

3 tablespoons milk

3 tablespoons butter

2 cups sour cream

10 ounces sharp Cheddar cheese, grated (about 2½ cups)

1 tablespoon garlic salt

Salt and pepper

6 slices bacon, cooked and crumbled

½ cup finely chopped green onion

Preheat the oven to 400°F.

Wash the potatoes and pierce them with a fork. Rub the potatoes with the olive oil and place them on a jellyroll pan or a large cookie sheet with a rim. Bake the potatoes for 45 minutes to an hour, or until done. Remove the potatoes from the oven and cut them in half lengthwise. Set aside. Reduce the temperature of the oven to 350°F.

When the potatoes are cool enough to handle, scoop out the potato flesh into a large electric mixing bowl. Add the milk, butter, sour cream, cheese, garlic salt, and salt and pepper to taste. Mix until creamy. Divide the mixture evenly and spoon it back into the potato shells. Return the potatoes to the oven for 15 minutes. Remove from the oven and garnish with the bacon and green onion.

I learned the hard way not to wrap the potatoes in foil before baking. It softens the shells and they will fall apart — not good! Baking them unwrapped makes the shells stronger for scooping out the potato flesh later.

cabbage casserole

I love cabbage! I love it raw or steamed, in slaw—you name it. I grew up going to lots of church family night suppers and school fund-raisers. There was almost always some kind of cabbage dish at these events, but I don't remember ever having anything that tasted this good. There probably isn't a more decadent way to serve cabbage! It would be good with other vegetables, such as broccoli or asparagus. Try your favorite. SERVES 10

1 medium head green cabbage

½ cup water

6 slices bacon, cooked and crumbled

1 cup mayonnaise

8 ounces sharp Cheddar cheese, grated (about 2 cups)

1 10-ounce can cream of chicken soup

2 large eggs, beaten

1 teaspoon salt

½ teaspoon pepper

40 butter crackers, such as Ritz, crushed

¼ cup (½ stick) butter, melted

Preheat the oven to 350°F. Spray a 9 × 12 × 2-inch baking dish with cooking spray.

Cut the cabbage in half, then lay each half flat side down and cut each section into eighths. In a large saucepan over medium heat, add the chopped cabbage and the water, and steam the cabbage just until wilted, about 5 minutes. Set the pan off the heat. Drain the cabbage. Add the crumbled bacon, mayonnaise, cheese, soup, eggs, salt, and pepper and stir together until completely mixed. Pour the mixture into the prepared dish. In a small bowl, combine the cracker crumbs with the melted butter, then sprinkle over the top of the cabbage mixture. Bake for 30 minutes, or until lightly browned on top.

potato casserole

Whenever I ask my children for menu suggestions, they always say mashed potatoes. I think they would eat mashed potatoes with anything! The only problem in our house is that nobody likes them cold, and on the rare occasion when we have leftovers, they usually sit in the refrigerator until I throw them out. In this recipe, the potatoes stay creamy and it's an easy dish to warm up in the microwave. You can even make it ahead of time and pop it into the oven at the last minute. **SERVES 8**

6 large russet potatoes

1 tablespoon salt

8 slices bacon

¼ cup (½ stick) butter

½ cup mayonnaise

½ cup sour cream

1 cup milk

8 ounces Cheddar cheese, grated (about 2 cups)

½ teaspoon garlic salt

½ teaspoon pepper

Preheat the oven to 400°F. Grease a 2-quart baking dish.

Peel the potatoes and cut them into 1-inch cubes. Place the potatoes and salt in a large saucepan with water to cover and bring to a boil. Reduce the heat and simmer the potatoes until very tender, about 30 minutes.

While the potatoes boil, cook the bacon in a medium skillet or in the microwave. Drain the bacon on paper towels and, when cool enough to handle, crumble it into small pieces. Set aside.

Drain the potatoes and transfer them to a large mixing bowl. Add the butter, mayonnaise, sour cream, milk, and half of the cheese to the potatoes. Add the garlic salt and pepper. Use an electric mixer to whip the potato mixture until thoroughly combined and spoon into the prepared baking dish. Sprinkle the crumbled bacon and the remaining cheese over the top and bake for 20 minutes, or until the cheese is melted and the casserole is heated through.

You can cook the potatoes faster if you use a pressure cooker. Cook the potatoes for about 5 minutes.

baked bean casserole

I'm always saying, "Simple is better!" I have made simple baked beans as a side ever since I began cooking twenty years ago. This recipe came from Beth's friend Gail Shoup. The dish quickly became the new baked bean side at our house. It is hearty enough for a meal. Garth loves a smoked barbecue sauce that our friend Charlie Nichols makes and brings to him on a regular basis. Garth calls it Charlie-que Sauce! It's a secret recipe that Charlie got from his grandmother. I use Charlie-que Sauce in these beans because it's Garth's favorite, but any thick barbecue sauce will do. Maybe someday I'll get Charlie's secret recipe! SERVES 12

1½ pounds lean ground beef

1 small onion, finely chopped

1 bell pepper, cored, seeded, and finely chopped

2 16-ounce cans pork and beans

½ cup barbecue sauce

½ cup ketchup

2 tablespoons spicy brown mustard

2 tablespoons Worcestershire sauce

1 tablespoon soy sauce

4 tablespoons brown sugar

6 to 8 slices bacon, cooked and crumbled

Preheat the oven to 350°F. Spray a 9 × 13 × 2-inch casserole dish with cooking spray.

In a large saucepan, brown the ground beef, onion, and bell pepper. Add the pork and beans, barbecue sauce, ketchup, mustard, Worcestershire sauce, soy sauce, and brown sugar to the mixture. Simmer for 5 minutes. Transfer the mixture to the prepared casserole dish. Crumble the bacon over the top of the casserole. Cover the dish with aluminum foil and bake for 45 minutes. Remove the foil and continue to bake for an additional 10 minutes. Let the casserole stand for 10 minutes before serving.

These beans go great with Fred's Barbecued Pork Ribs (page 99).

cranberry-orange relish

We've always served the traditional canned cranberry sauce (one of my nephew Kyle's favorite food groups) at Thanksgiving and Christmas, but a couple of years ago, Beth's friend Vicki Walker brought us this delicious mixture of fresh oranges, cranberries, and nuts. We still open a can for Kyle (and, let's be honest, for Aunt Trisha), but everybody else loves this stuff. Kyle and I are just old school. **MAKES 2 CUPS**

1 12-ounce package fresh cranberries

2 oranges, peeled

1 cup sugar

½ cup pecans, finely chopped

Using a food processor, pulse the cranberries and oranges. Transfer the chopped fruit to a 1-quart bowl and add ½ cup of sugar, stirring to mix. Add more sugar to taste, as the sweetness of the oranges will vary. Add the chopped pecans and serve.

> FROM GWEN: This relish will keep for up to 2 weeks in the refrigerator (if it doesn't disappear before then!).

sweet potato pudding

I meet a lot of people who say they didn't think they liked sweet potatoes–until they tried them prepared in a different way from just baked and topped with butter and brown sugar. I happen to love sweet potatoes any way they're prepared, but this pudding is a good alternative for those who don't care for the potato plain. This has lots of flavor and is a great side dish for Thanksgiving. SERVES 8

2½ pounds (about 3) medium sweet potatoes

½ cup (1 stick) butter, room temperature

2 large eggs

1 tablespoon self-rising cornmeal

1 cup sugar

½ cup milk

¼ teaspoon salt

1 teaspoon vanilla extract

1 cup pecan halves

½ cup packed brown sugar

This dish can be topped with whipped cream and eaten for dessert!

Preheat the oven to 400°F. Spray an 8-inch square baking dish with cooking spray.

On a foil-covered baking sheet, bake the sweet potatoes for 1 hour, or until they are soft. Remove and let cool. Reduce the heat of the oven to 325°F. When cool enough to handle, peel the

This was brought to the Paulk family reunion by my great aunt Ora's daughter, Pat Sizemore Foster.

FROM GWEN: The top of this pudding should be browned, but watch to make sure you don't burn the pecans.

potatoes, place the flesh in a large mixing bowl, add the butter, and mash until smooth. Add the eggs, one at a time, beating well after each addition. Add the cornmeal, sugar, milk, salt, and ½ teaspoon of the vanilla and beat until smooth. Pour the batter into the prepared baking dish. Arrange the pecan halves on top of the pudding and top with the brown sugar. Sprinkle the remaining ½ teaspoon vanilla by small droplets over the brown sugar. Bake for 45 minutes, or until the top is browned.

homemade whipped cream MAKES 3 OR 4 CUPS

2 cups (1 pint) whipping cream, chilled in the refrigerator

4 tablespoons sugar

FROM GWEN: Beating times and the amount produced may differ depending on the temperature of the bowl and the cream.

FROM GWEN: Leftover whipped cream will separate slightly when stored in the refrigerator, but may be whipped again.

Chill a large metal mixing bowl and the wire beater attachment in the freezer for about 20 minutes.

Pour the chilled cream into the cold mixing bowl and beat until it forms soft mounds, about 10 minutes. Reduce the mixer speed, stirring as you add the sugar by tablespoonfuls. Continue beating until the cream forms more defined peaks, about 5 minutes. The mixture should hold its shape when dropped from a spoon. Don't overbeat or you'll have sweetened butter!

breads

A meal isn't complete without bread! I try to serve some sort of bread at every home-cooked meal. These rolls and breads are good on their own, or served crumbled up underneath a rich soup or chili. The sweet breads in this chapter are a welcome addition to a morning cup of coffee or served as a light dessert after supper.

easiest muffins

For those of you who, like me, are a little intimidated by the idea of making biscuits from scratch, try these muffins. Somehow when you call them muffins, they sound easier! They're sometimes called 2-2-1 muffins or drop biscuits, but whatever you call them, they're quick and easy. These are great right out of the oven as is or served with soup on a cold winter day. This recipe came from family friend Mary Lou Jordan.   **SERVES 12**

1 cup (2 sticks) margarine, softened

1 cup sour cream

2 cups self-rising flour

Preheat the oven to 400°F. In an electric mixer, mix the margarine and sour cream. Add the flour and mix well. Drop large spoonfuls of the dough into a muffin pan that has been sprayed with cooking spray or lined with muffin cups. Bake for 25 minutes, or until the tops of the muffins are golden brown.

> FROM GWEN: For smaller muffins, use mini muffin pans and reduce the baking time to 15 minutes.

After adding the flour, add 1/2 cup grated Cheddar cheese and 1/4 teaspoon garlic powder for cheesy muffins.

spoon rolls

My cousin on my daddy's side of the family Peggy Leach shared this really easy recipe. Mix the batter to keep in the refrigerator, and you can have hot rolls at a moment's notice.

MAKES 5 DOZEN MINI ROLLS

¼ ounce (1 packet) active dry yeast

2 cups warm (100°F) water

¾ cup (1½ sticks) butter, melted

¼ cup sugar

1 large egg

4 cups self-rising flour

Dissolve the yeast in the warm water. Mix the butter and sugar with an electric mixer. Beat in the egg. Add the yeast and mix well. Gradually stir in the flour, until smooth. Pour into a 2-quart, greased, airtight bowl. Store tightly covered in the refrigerator overnight.

The next day, preheat the oven to 350°F. Grease miniature muffin tins.

Spoon the dough into the muffin tins and bake the rolls for 18 to 20 minutes, or until browned.

FROM GWEN: The batter will rise in the refrigerator. Do not punch down. Just dip by large spoonfuls to fill muffin cups. Any remaining batter can be stored in the refrigerator for a couple more days.

FROM BETH: The batter may become thinner on the second day. Just stir it and add a bit more flour if needed.

sour cream cornbread

We've been preparing and sharing many of the recipes in this book for generations, so it's a big deal when I find something new that I like. I *flipped* over this cornbread! I still make my basic cornbread, but when I'm making a winter soup or chili, I now make this hearty version to go along with it. It's also good right out of the oven, topped with a little butter. (Let's face it—what isn't?) **SERVES 8**

1¼ cups self-rising buttermilk cornmeal mix

1 15-ounce can creamed corn

1 cup sour cream

¼ cup vegetable oil

3 large eggs

Preheat the oven to 450°F. Spray a well-seasoned 10-inch cast-iron skillet with cooking spray.

In a medium mixing bowl, combine the cornmeal mix, creamed corn, sour cream, oil, and eggs. Pour the mixture into the skillet and bake for 30 minutes, or until lightly brown.

This cornbread is great served with Fancy Chili (page 64).

margaret's raisin bread

My fourth-grade teacher made this in 1-pound coffee cans as gifts for her children's teachers back in the '70s. I got her recipe for my mom. Mom still has it in her recipe file, handwritten by me. MAKES 3 MINI LOAVES

1 cup boiling water

1½ cups raisins

2 teaspoons baking soda

1½ cups all-purpose flour

1 cup sugar

¼ teaspoon salt

1 cup crushed bran flakes

1 large egg

¼ cup vegetable oil

NOTE: To bake in cans, heavily grease and flour the insides of three 16-ounce cans.

Preheat the oven to 350°F. Prepare three 6 × 3 × 2-inch miniature loaf pans by greasing them and lining the bottoms with parchment paper (see Note).

In a medium heatproof mixing bowl, pour the boiling water over the raisins and baking soda. Set aside to cool.

In a medium mixing bowl, sift together the flour, sugar, and salt. Stir in the bran flake crumbs. Lightly beat together the egg and oil, and stir into the flour mixture. Stir in the cooled raisins and water. Divide the batter evenly among the three pans. Bake for about 30 minutes, or until a toothpick inserted in the center comes out clean. Cool in the pans for about 10 minutes, then turn out onto racks for cooling.

FROM BETH: My children love to bake in a can!

cranberry bread

I love sweet-tasting breads. They're a nice alternative to dessert. They're also a great addition to a salad or a substitution for morning toast. I love this bread for a late-afternoon snack, toasted, topped with a dab of butter, and served with a fresh cup of coffee. **MAKES 1 LOAF**

2 cups all-purpose flour

1½ teaspoons baking powder

½ teaspoon baking soda

½ teaspoon salt

1 cup sugar

2 teaspoons grated orange zest

½ cup fresh orange juice

¼ cup warm water

1 large egg

2 tablespoons butter, melted

1 cup walnuts, finely chopped

1 cup fresh cranberries, chopped

Preheat the oven to 350°F. Spray a 9 × 5-inch loaf pan with cooking spray.

Sift together the flour, baking powder, baking soda, salt, and sugar. In a large mixing bowl, combine the orange zest, orange juice, water, egg, and butter. Add the flour mixture to the egg mixture and mix until the ingredients are just blended. With a spatula, fold in the walnuts and cranberries. Pour the batter into the prepared pan. Bake for 1 hour. Cool in the pan for 10 minutes, then turn out onto a cooling rack.

My friend Melissa adds 8 ounces of white chocolate chips to this recipe. Yum!

pat's pumpkin bread

Pat McCormack makes this pumpkin bread every Christmas. That's how I got my first taste of this awesome treat. She makes mini loaves in cute porcelain pans, wraps them in red and green cellophane, and gives them as gifts. The only problem is that she lives in California. Her daughter, Mandy, a good friend of mine, decided that we shouldn't wait to get these in the mail from her mom, so she made a batch this past Halloween for us to enjoy. By the way, Miss Pat, this doesn't get you out of making me some for Christmas.

MAKES 3 LOAVES

1 cup vegetable oil

3 cups sugar

4 large eggs

1 15-ounce can pumpkin

3½ cups all-purpose flour

½ teaspoon baking powder

2 teaspoons baking soda

1 teaspoon ground cinnamon

1 teaspoon ground allspice

1 teaspoon salt

1 teaspoon ground cloves

²/₃ cup water

½ cup walnuts, finely chopped

Preheat the oven to 350°F. Spray three 9 × 5-inch loaf pans with cooking spray.

In an electric mixer, beat the oil, sugar, eggs, and pumpkin until smooth. Sift together the flour, baking powder, baking soda, cinnamon, allspice, salt, and cloves. Add the flour mixture and the water to the egg mixture, alternating flour and water and beginning and ending with the flour mixture. Fold in the walnuts. Pour into the loaf pans and bake for 1 hour and 10 minutes, or until a toothpick inserted into the center of each loaf comes out clean.

zucchini bread

If you've ever planted a vegetable garden in the South, then you know that a few zucchini plants go a long way. Now, we love zucchini, but once you've eaten it steamed, fried, and sautéed, and you're still giving it away, it's nice to have a sweet alternative! This quick-bread recipe combines the humble zucchini with cinnamon, coconut, and even maraschino cherries. There's more than one way to eat your veggies. **MAKES 2 LOAVES**

3 cups all-purpose flour

1 teaspoon salt

1 teaspoon baking soda

1 teaspoon baking powder

1 teaspoon ground cinnamon

3 large eggs, beaten

1 cup vegetable oil

2 cups sugar

3 cups grated zucchini

½ cup frozen grated coconut, thawed

½ cup walnuts, chopped

¼ cup maraschino cherries

Preheat the oven to 325°F. Grease two 5 × 9-inch loaf pans with cooking spray.

In a mixing bowl, sift together the flour, salt, baking soda, baking powder, and cinnamon. Mix the beaten eggs, oil, and sugar and add to the flour mixture. Stir in the grated zucchini, coconut, nuts, and cherries. Pour the batter into the loaf pans and bake for 1 hour; a toothpick inserted into the center of the loaf should come out clean. Cool for 10 minutes before removing the loaves from the pans. Turn the breads out onto wire racks to cool completely.

broccoli cornbread

At some southern restaurants, you'll always be given a choice of biscuits or cornbread. It's a no-brainer for me. I like biscuits, but I *love* cornbread, so the more varieties I can come up with, the better. My mom's neighbor Elizabeth Davis shared a pan of this with us. She and I are several years apart in age, but our families were neighbors growing up, and sometimes we would give her a ride to school in the mornings. Elizabeth's a grown woman now with children of her own, but to me she'll always be that little eight-year-old girl riding to school with us! SERVES 8

3 tablespoons corn oil

1½ cups self-rising buttermilk cornbread mix

½ cup chopped sweet onion, such as Vidalia

10 ounces pepper Jack cheese, grated (about 2½ cups)

8 ounces (2 cups) fresh broccoli florets, chopped

½ teaspoon black pepper

1 jalapeño pepper, seeded and chopped

1 cup sour cream

¾ cup buttermilk

2 tablespoons butter, melted

Preheat the oven to 350°F.

Put the corn oil in a 9-inch heavy cast-iron skillet that has been well seasoned to prevent sticking (see Note).

In a large bowl, mix the cornbread mix, onion, cheese, broccoli, black pepper, and jalapeño pepper. Stir in the sour cream, buttermilk, and melted butter to make a thick batter.

Heat the oil in the skillet and spoon in the batter, pressing it evenly to the edge. Oil will come up around the edges of the skillet. Spread this oil over the top of the batter to make the bread brown. Bake for 45 minutes. Cool in the pan for 10 minutes, then carefully loosen the edges and bottom with an egg turner. Put the bread on a rack to cool.

NOTE: This bread is very soft and may stick to a skillet that is not well seasoned. If this happens, cut the bread out of the skillet in serving portions.

FROM BETH: Four thinly sliced yellow squash may be substituted for the broccoli.

jalapeño hushpuppies

Jalapeños are one of my favorite things to use to spice up a recipe. Fresh jalapeños are the best and have less sodium than canned—but canned works, too! The corn makes these hushpuppies really moist. If you're cooking up a "mess" of fish, try these alongside Pete's Catfish (page 109). **MAKES ABOUT 36**

1½ quarts peanut oil

1½ cups self-rising cornmeal

1 cup self-rising flour

½ cup chopped onion

1 7-ounce can diced jalapeño peppers, drained, or ¾ cup fresh jalapeños, seeded and finely diced

1 15-ounce can creamed corn

2 large eggs, lightly beaten

Salt

Heat the oil to 350°F in a deep fryer or Dutch oven.

In a 1-quart mixing bowl, stir the cornmeal, flour, onion, jalapeño, corn, and eggs until blended. Allow to stand for 5 minutes.

Drop the batter by teaspoonfuls into the hot oil. Don't overcrowd; leave room for the hushpuppies to be turned. Cook the hushpuppies to a golden brown, about 3 minutes. Remove from the oil with a slotted spoon and drain on paper towels. Keep the cooked hushpuppies warm in the oven while cooking the rest of the batter. Lightly salt to taste before serving.

blanche's miniature cherry muffins

Blanche Bernard is Beth's mother-in-law. This is the first recipe that Blanche gave Beth after Beth and John married. (She also gave the mini-muffin tins that Beth still uses twenty-four years later to bake them.) My nine-year-old nephew Bret had these for the first time recently and said, "Cherries have never really been my pleasure, but these muffins are good!" The boy has a way with words! MAKES 36 TO 40 MUFFINS

¼ cup butter, room temperature

½ cup brown sugar

½ cup granulated sugar

2 eggs yolks, well beaten

1 cup all-purpose flour

¼ teaspoon baking powder

1 10-ounce jar maraschino cherries, drained, juices reserved

2 egg whites, stiffly beaten

½ cup chopped pecans

Powdered sugar for dusting

Preheat the oven to 400°F. Grease the cups of 2 mini-muffin tins and set aside. Cream the butter and brown and granulated sugars. Add the beaten egg yolks, flour, baking powder and 2 tablespoons of the cherry juice, blending well. Fold in the egg whites. Sprinkle ¼ teaspoon of chopped nuts in the bottom of each muffin cup. Spoon in 1 teaspoon of batter, then place half a cherry in the center of the batter. Drop another teaspoon of batter on top. Sprinkle a few chopped nuts on top of each muffin. Bake for 10 minutes, then remove from the tins and dust with powdered sugar while hot.

FROM BETH: Using a measuring spoon to measure the batter will keep the muffin cups from running over. They are good with or without the powdered sugar coating.

cakes and pies

Most people have dessert as the sweet reward after a satisfying supper. I tend to save dessert for an afternoon snack with coffee, so that I can be hungry for it and then savor every bite.

There's something for everyone in this chapter. Our daughter August isn't a chocolate fan (insert audible gasp here!). I usually make an alternative for her when I'm baking a chocolate dessert. From Key Lime Cake (page 161) to Magic Lemon Meringue Pie (page 187), there are lots of choices for those who don't like to wallow in chocolate, like most of us!

fresh apple cake

I was intrigued by this recipe because I couldn't imagine how it would turn out. The Bundt pan makes it really pretty, so it's a nice cake to take to a party or family gathering. The cinnamon and walnuts give it a spicy, holiday flavor. SERVES 10 TO 12

CAKE

2 cups sugar

3 large eggs

1½ cups vegetable oil

½ cup orange juice, regular or fresh

3 cups all-purpose flour

½ teaspoon salt

1 teaspoon baking soda

½ teaspoon ground cinnamon

1 teaspoon vanilla extract

1 cup walnuts, finely chopped

2½ cups peeled, cored, and finely diced sweet apples (about 4 medium apples)

GLAZE

6 tablespoons (¾ stick) butter

¾ cup sugar

½ teaspoon baking soda

⅓ cup buttermilk

Preheat the oven to 325°F. Thoroughly grease a 10-inch Bundt pan with Crisco and lightly flour it.

With an electric mixer, beat the sugar, eggs, and oil until smooth. Add the orange juice and mix well. Sift together the flour, salt, baking soda, and cinnamon. Add the flour mixture to the sugar mixture and beat well. Add the vanilla. Stir in the walnuts and apples, until blended. Pour the batter into the pan. Bake for 1 hour and 30 minutes. Remove the cake from the oven, let it cool in the pan for 15 minutes, then turn out onto a cake plate.

For the glaze, combine the butter, sugar, baking soda, and buttermilk in a large saucepan and bring to a boil. Boil the mixture for 5 to 10 minutes, until it thickens slightly and begins to turn light brown. Take off the heat. Using a toothpick, punch 15 or 20 holes in the top of the cake and pour the glaze over the cake. Let the cake set and cool before serving. Store the cake in an airtight cake carrier in the refrigerator for up to 2 weeks.

> FROM GWEN: Cakes baked in Bundt pans tend to stick, so liberally grease and flour your pan for a perfect cake.

lizzie's strawberry cake

I always think homemade has to mean strictly from scratch, so I tried every way I could think of to make this strawberry cake without using a cake mix! I even used a homemade white cake in place of the mix. It tasted good, but not any better than this recipe. When I found my grandmother Lizzie Paulk's original recipe from the 1930s, and saw it had a cake mix in it, I thought to myself, "Well, that makes it okay!" If you love strawberries as much as I do, you're in for a real treat. **SERVES 12**

CAKE

1 standard box plain white cake mix

1 3-ounce box strawberry-flavored gelatin

⅔ cup vegetable oil

½ cup frozen sliced strawberries in syrup, thawed

½ cup water

4 large eggs

ICING

½ cup (1 stick) butter, room temperature

1 cup confectioners' sugar

1 cup frozen sliced strawberries in syrup, thawed

Preheat the oven to 350°F. Spray a 9 × 13 × 2-inch baking pan with cooking spray.

With an electric mixer, beat the cake mix, gelatin, oil, strawberries, and water until fully combined. Add the eggs, one at a time, beating well after each addition. Pour the batter into the prepared pan and gently smooth the top. Bake for 40 minutes, or until a toothpick inserted in the center of the cake comes out clean. Let cool in the pan.

In a blender or food processor, puree the butter, sugar, and strawberries for the glaze until smooth. Poke holes in the cake with a toothpick, then pour the icing over the cake, allowing some of it to seep into the cake. The more strawberry syrup you add, the thinner your icing will become. Store this cake, covered, in the refrigerator for up to 2 weeks.

Serve this cake right out of the pan!

key lime cake

We had a big birthday party for my daddy when he turned seventy. He was a pretty humble guy and was embarrassed that so much attention was being focused on him, but he ultimately loved visiting with all of his friends, some he hadn't seen in a long time. Over two hundred friends and family signed the guest book that night; that's a testament to the man. I think of him when I make this cake because we served it that night. I miss my daddy, but there are always things to remind me of how much fun we had as a family.

SERVES 12

CAKE

1 3-ounce package lime-flavored gelatin

1⅓ cups granulated sugar

2 cups sifted all-purpose flour

½ teaspoon salt

1 teaspoon baking powder

1 teaspoon baking soda

5 large eggs, slightly beaten

1½ cups vegetable oil

¾ cup orange juice

1 tablespoon lemon juice

½ teaspoon vanilla extract

½ cup Key lime juice (from about 25 small Key limes or 4 large regular limes)

½ cup confectioners' sugar

Preheat the oven to 350°F. Grease and flour three 9-inch round cake pans.

In a large mixing bowl, mix the gelatin, sugar, flour, salt, baking powder, and baking soda. Stir to mix well. Add the eggs, oil, orange juice, lemon juice, and vanilla. Divide the batter evenly among the 3 pans and bake for 35 to 40 minutes. Test for doneness by lightly touching the tops of the layers or inserting a toothpick. Cool the layers in the pans for 5 minutes, then turn them out onto racks.

While the layers are still hot, mix the lime juice and confectioners' sugar and pour it over the layers on the racks. You can pierce the layers with a fork to allow the glaze to soak in better. Allow the layers to cool completely as you prepare the icing.

recipe continues

FROM BETH: This is a very moist cake. It can also be baked in a 9 x 12 x 2-inch pan to be easily served in squares.

FROM GWEN: This recipe comes from family friend Angela Spivey. She uses whichever variety of lime is available in the local grocery.

CREAM CHEESE ICING

½ cup (1 stick) butter, room temperature

1 8-ounce package cream cheese, room temperature

1 1-pound box confectioners' sugar

Cream the butter and cream cheese. Beat in the confectioners' sugar until the mixture is smooth and easy to spread. Spread the icing between the layers and on the top and sides of the cake.

The cream cheese icing is optional. This cake is beautiful and tastes great with just the glaze poured over it.

Key limes can be hard to find. Substitute regular lime juice for Key lime juice without sacrificing flavor.

cold-oven pound cake

My dad's aunt Marie had eight children to rear during the Great Depression. Starting a cake in a cold oven was just one way to save on fuel at a time when every penny counted. Times have changed, but I like to make this cake the way Great-Aunt Marie did, and try to imagine what it must have been like to be a mother to eight children. Maybe I'll just preheat the oven! **SERVES 15**

1 cup (2 sticks) butter, room temperature

3 cups sugar

6 large eggs, room temperature

3 cups all-purpose flour, sifted

1 cup heavy whipping cream

1 teaspoon vanilla extract

Do not preheat the oven. Grease and flour the bottom, sides, and tube of a 9-inch tube cake pan.

Cream the butter and sugar until smooth. Add the eggs, one at a time, mixing well after each addition, but do not overbeat. Set the mixer on slow speed and stir in the flour and cream alternately, beginning and ending with the flour. Add the vanilla and stir well. Pour the batter into the prepared pan and put the cake in a cold oven. Set the oven temperature to 325°F. Begin timing now and bake the cake for 1 hour and 15 minutes. Test for doneness by inserting a toothpick in the center of the cake. The toothpick should be clean when it is removed. Cool in the pan for 30 minutes, then turn out onto a rack to continue cooling.

Great-Aunt Marie Yearwood Bruce, my grandaddy Bo's sister, in her cucumber patch.

old-fashioned strawberry shortcake

I'm a fan of salt and sweet mixed together. My grandmother Lizzie Paulk often used biscuits in place of pastry in her recipes. Nowadays, most people use angel food cake or pound cake for this dessert, but I like the old-fashioned mix of the not-so-sweet biscuit with the sweetness of the strawberries and the whipped cream. I serve this dessert in the summer with fresh-picked berries from our local strawberry farm. SERVES 8 TO 10

4 cups sifted all-purpose flour

2 tablespoons baking powder

1 teaspoon salt

1¼ cups plus 2 tablespoons sugar

⅔ cup butter (11 tablespoons), cold and cut into small pieces

2 large eggs, beaten

1 cup milk

2 tablespoons butter, melted

3 pints fresh strawberries

1 cup heavy cream, whipped

Preheat the oven to 450°F. Grease the bottoms of two 9-inch round cake pans.

In a large mixing bowl, sift together the flour, baking powder, salt, and ½ cup of the sugar. Add the butter and cut in with 2 knives or a pastry blender to coarse-crumb consistency. In a large bowl, beat the eggs. Add the milk until fully combined. Gradually stir the egg and milk mixture into the flour mixture. Knead the dough for about 20 seconds on a lightly floured board. Pat half the dough into each cake pan. Brush the surfaces with melted butter. Bake for 12 to 15 minutes, until lightly browned. Turn the shortcake layers out onto cooling racks.

While the layers are cooling, wash the strawberries and remove the hulls. Reserve a few berries for garnish. Cut the large berries in half and sprinkle with ¾ cup of the sugar. Let stand for about 30 minutes.

Spoon half of the berries with their juice over one shortcake layer. Place the second layer on top and spoon the remaining berries and juice over it. Sprinkle with the remaining 2 tablespoons sugar and top with the whipped cream.

carrot cake

My friend Tana first made this cake and left it in our refrigerator for us to enjoy when we returned home from a trip. What a sweet surprise, literally! This cake has become a regular dessert at our house and a popular request for birthdays. I think what makes it unique is that it is cut into six layers. The pureed carrots make for a smoother cake. Of course, at my house, nobody cares about that, they just think it's good! SERVES 12

CAKE

3 cups granulated sugar

1½ cups corn oil

4 large eggs

1 tablespoon vanilla extract

3 cups all-purpose flour

1 tablespoon baking soda

1 tablespoon ground cinnamon

1 teaspoon salt

1½ cups walnuts, finely chopped

1½ cups frozen grated coconut, thawed

1½ cups pureed carrots (about 6 medium, boiled)

¾ cup crushed pineapple, drained

Preheat the oven to 350°F. Grease the bottom of three 9-inch round cake pans with cooking spray, line with circles of parchment paper, and grease the paper with cooking spray.

With an electric mixer, cream the sugar, oil, eggs, and vanilla. Sift together the flour, baking soda, cinnamon, and salt. Add the dry ingredients to the sugar mixture. Add the walnuts, coconut, carrot puree, and pineapple, and beat until smooth. Divide the batter evenly among the prepared pans and bake for 40 to 45 minutes, or until a toothpick inserted into the center comes out clean.

Cool the layers in the pans for about 5 minutes. Run a knife around the edges of each pan and turn the layers out onto wire racks that have been sprayed with cooking spray. Cool the layers completely before frosting (see Note).

NOTE: After the layers have cooled, wrap each in plastic wrap and refrigerate overnight. They are easier to handle and cut in half the next day. Also, to handle as little as possible, put the first layer of cake on the plate you intend to store it on, slice it in half, ease a piece of parchment between the layers, and lift the top portion off. Frost the bottom slice, and then add the next layer. Continue until the entire cake is frosted.

recipe continues

CREAM CHEESE FROSTING

2 8-ounce packages cream cheese, room temperature

¾ cup (1½ sticks) butter, room temperature

6 cups confectioners' sugar

2 teaspoons vanilla extract

2 cups walnuts, finely chopped

To make the frosting, combine the cream cheese and butter in an electric mixer and beat until smooth. Slowly add the confectioners' sugar and continue beating until fully combined. Add the vanilla.

Slice each layer horizontally in half using an electric knife. Frost each layer, the sides, and the top of the cake. Press the chopped walnuts into the sides of the cake. Refrigerate until ready to serve.

grandma yearwood's coconut cake
with coconut lemon glaze

We found this recipe in my grandma's recipe file. I thought it was interesting because I'd never made a cake with vanilla wafer crumbs. For years my mom made a more difficult divinity icing for her coconut cakes, only to learn much later that my dad actually preferred the juicier, easier glaze that his mother made. I was really happy to find this recipe because I thought it had been lost forever and I had heard about this legendary cake all my life! **SERVES 12**

CAKE

1 cup (2 sticks) butter, room temperature

2 cups sugar

6 large eggs, room temperature

1 teaspoon vanilla extract

1 12-ounce box vanilla wafers, finely crushed

1 6-ounce package frozen grated coconut, thawed

½ cup chopped pecans

COCONUT LEMON GLAZE

2 cups sugar

2 tablespoons cornstarch

Pinch of salt

Grated zest of 2 large lemons

¼ cup fresh lemon juice (juice of about 2 large lemons)

1½ cups water

1 6-ounce package frozen grated coconut, thawed

Preheat the oven to 325°F. Grease and flour a 9-inch tube cake pan.

Cream the butter and sugar until light and smooth. Add the eggs and vanilla, beating well. Mix in the vanilla wafer crumbs, coconut, and pecans. Pour into the pan and bake for 1 hour and 15 minutes. Allow the cake to cool in the pan for 10 minutes before turning out onto a rack.

For the glaze, mix the sugar, cornstarch, salt, lemon zest and juice, water, and coconut in a medium saucepan. Cook over medium heat, stirring until thickened, about 15 minutes. Let cool slightly, then, using a toothpick, poke several holes in the top of the cake and drizzle the glaze over the cake.

Grandma Yearwood, Beth, and me, 1967.

spice cake with lemon sauce

My memory of this spice cake is of coming home from school and slicing a piece right out of the pan, putting a little lemon sauce on it, warming it up in the microwave for a few seconds, then sitting down to watch a M*A*S*H rerun on television before I had to start my homework. Heaven! We used a really tangy lemon sauce for years, but our longtime family friend Miss Betty Maxwell turned us on to this sweeter version of the sauce and it's so good. I make this cake at the first sign of fall. The smell of it baking in the house gets me excited because I know Thanksgiving and Christmas are right around the corner!

MAKES ABOUT 22 (2-INCH) SQUARES

CAKE

2½ cups sifted self-rising flour

1 teaspoon baking soda

¾ teaspoon ground cinnamon

½ teaspoon ground cloves

1 cup granulated sugar

⅔ cup light brown sugar

⅔ cup vegetable shortening, such as Crisco

2 large eggs, room temperature

1 cup buttermilk

LEMON SAUCE

3 large eggs

2 cups granulated sugar

Juice of 3 lemons

Grated zest of 1 lemon

1 cup (2 sticks) butter, cut into ½-inch cubes

Preheat the oven to 350°F. Grease and flour the bottom of a 9 × 13 × 2-inch baking pan.

Sift together the flour, baking soda, cinnamon, and cloves. With an electric mixer, cream the sugars with the shortening. Add the eggs, one at a time, beating after each addition. Add the buttermilk alternately with the flour mixture, beginning and ending with flour, stirring until no flour is visible. Don't overbeat. Spread the batter into the pan and bake for 35 to 40 minutes. Test for doneness by inserting a toothpick into the center of the cake. If the toothpick comes out clean, the cake is done. Cool the cake slightly in the pan and turn out onto a long rack while still warm.

To make the sauce, whisk the eggs and sugar over medium heat in the top of a double boiler. Stir in the lemon juice, zest, and butter. Cook the mixture until it thickens, about 30 minutes.

Cut the spice cake into squares and serve warm with lemon sauce.

> FROM BETH: The lemon sauce may be stored in the refrigerator for up to 1 week.

red velvet cake

This recipe came from Mrs. Gail Sealy. She taught first grade at my school, alongside my mom, who taught third grade for twenty-three years. Before we knew her, my sister and I called "Miss" Sealy the movie star lady because she was, and still is, stunningly beautiful and had this exotic look about her. She also drank Tab all the time. I thought she was the coolest! I don't think she drinks Tab anymore, but I still think she's cool. SERVES 12

CAKE

2½ cups all-purpose flour

1 teaspoon baking soda

1 teaspoon salt

2 teaspoons unsweetened cocoa powder

2 cups granulated sugar

2 large eggs

1¾ cups vegetable oil

1 cup buttermilk

1 teaspoon vanilla extract

1 2-ounce bottle red food coloring

CREAM CHEESE FROSTING

1 8-ounce package cream cheese, room temperature

½ cup (1 stick) butter, room temperature

1 1-pound box confectioners' sugar

1 teaspoon vanilla extract

1 cup pecans, finely chopped

Preheat the oven to 350°F. Grease and flour three 9-inch round cake pans.

Sift together the flour, baking soda, salt, and cocoa. Mix the sugar and eggs. Add the oil, slowly beating well as the oil is added. Add the flour mixture alternately with the buttermilk, beginning and ending with the flour and mixing well after each addition. Stir in the vanilla and food coloring. Divide the batter evenly among the pans and bake for 40 minutes, testing for doneness with a toothpick. Cool the layers in the pans for 10 minutes, then turn out onto racks to finish cooling while you prepare the frosting.

Cream the cream cheese and butter. Beat in the confectioners' sugar until the mixture is smooth. Add the vanilla and nuts, reserving 2 tablespoons of nuts for garnish. Spread the frosting between the layers, on the sides, and on the top of the cake.

FROM BETH: Leave the sides unfrosted if you like, to let the vibrant red show.

chocolate cake with divinity icing

I loved my grandaddy Paulk, my mom's dad. He always made us feel like we were the most special children in the world. When he and Grandma would come to visit, he had a smile for everybody and a laugh that was contagious. He loved a good meal. Grandma was such a wonderful cook, and she always had an amazing meal waiting for him when he would come in from working in the field or at the dairy barn. When he came to our house for his birthday, my mom would make this cake for him. **SERVES 12 TO 15**

1 cup water

2¼ cups sugar

4 ounces (4 squares) unsweetened chocolate

1½ teaspoons vanilla extract

3 cups cake flour, sifted

4½ teaspoons baking powder

¾ teaspoon salt

1 cup (2 sticks) butter, room temperature

4 large eggs, room temperature

¾ cup milk

Divinity Icing (recipe follows)

NOTE: The chocolate may be melted with ½ cup of sugar in 1 cup of water in the microwave.

FROM GWEN: My mother, Lizzie, used one large marshmallow for each egg white for perfect divinity icing.

In a small saucepan, combine the water, ½ cup of the sugar, and the chocolate. Heat over low heat, stirring constantly, until thick (see Note). Remove the pan from the heat and add the vanilla. Set aside to cool.

Preheat the oven to 350°F. Prepare three 9-inch round cake pans by greasing and lining each with parchment paper.

Sift the flour with the baking powder and salt onto waxed paper. Cream the butter and the remaining 1¾ cups sugar until smooth. Add the eggs, one at a time, beating after each addition. Add the cooled chocolate mixture and beat until smooth. Add the sifted flour mixture alternately with the milk, starting with a third of the flour, then adding half the milk, and ending with the flour. Stir only enough after each addition to blend the ingredients. Pour evenly into the pans and bake for 35 minutes, or until done. Judge doneness by appearance—layers will begin to pull away from the sides—or by inserting a toothpick in the center of a layer. The toothpick should come out clean. Cool in the pans for 10 minutes, then turn out onto racks. Remove the paper and cool completely before frosting. Spread the icing between the layers and on the top and sides of the cake.

recipe continues

Don't try this with a single-bladed mixer like KitchenAid; and don't make it on a rainy day because humidity can make it impossible to achieve perfect divinity.

divinity icing

MAKES ICING FOR THREE 9-INCH LAYERS

3 large egg whites, room
temperature

⅛ teaspoon salt

3 cups sugar

¾ cup water

3 tablespoons white corn syrup

¾ teaspoon white vinegar

30 miniature marshmallows
or 3 large marshmallows,
cut up

1½ teaspoons vanilla extract

Put the egg whites and salt in the bowl of a mixer that uses 2 beaters. Beat the whites until smooth but not stiff. They should not form stiff peaks when the beaters are lifted up.

In a large saucepan with a cover, mix the sugar, water, corn syrup, and vinegar. Stir until the sugar dissolves, then cover and cook for 3 minutes to melt any sugar crystals that may be on the sides of the saucepan. Remove the lid and continue cooking for about 12 minutes, until the mixture reaches the hard ball stage, about 265°F on a candy thermometer. The syrup will spin a long thread when poured from the edge of a spoon. Remove the syrup from the heat and stir in the marshmallows. The mixture will be foamy. With the mixer running at high speed, stream the syrup into the egg whites, following the groove the beaters make as the bowl turns. Beat well and add the vanilla.

Grandaddy Paulk helping me and Beth ice his birthday cake.

chocolate torte

Beth had never had a cake with this many layers before moving to South Georgia. Around there, it's known as twelve-layer chocolate cake, or seventeen-layer–almost a point of pride to see how many thin little layers you can get out of the recipe! At first glance, this cake screams, "Don't try this at home" because three layers is pretty much my limit. But Beth's friend Gail, who is known in those parts for her delicious food, shared her mother's recipe with us. Gail says that the older ladies in her community used to cook these layers one at a time on a cast-iron griddle. She's made it "easy" for us with 9-inch cake pans, so with her directions even I can bake a multilayer (twelve? thirteen? fifteen?) chocolate torte! SERVES 15

1¾ cups (3½ sticks) butter, 1 cup at room temperature

5 ounces (5 squares) unsweetened chocolate, melted

7 cups sugar

2¼ cups (18 ounces) evaporated milk

3 teaspoons vanilla extract

1 tablespoon instant French roast coffee granules

6 large eggs, room temperature

2 cups plus 1 tablespoon milk

4 cups self-rising flour

Make the cake glaze before baking the cake layers. In a large saucepan, melt ¾ cup of the butter and mix it with the melted chocolate and 4½ cups of the sugar. Stir in the evaporated milk, 2 teaspoons of the vanilla, and the instant coffee. Cook the glaze over medium-high heat until it boils. Reduce the heat to low and continue cooking, stirring constantly, until the mixture thickens, about 20 minutes. Remove the glaze from the heat. When cooled a bit, return to low heat as needed, as the glaze must be warm to spread on the cake layers.

Preheat the oven to 350°F. Grease and flour at least four 9-inch cake pans (see Note).

NOTE: Borrow pans from friends if you can in order to bake this special cake. You will be able to work quickly by having layers ready to bake while you frost the baked ones.

recipe continues

Cream the remaining 1 cup butter and remaining 2½ cups sugar until smooth. Add the eggs, one at a time, beating after each addition just until blended. Mix the remaining 1 teaspoon vanilla with the milk and add alternately with the flour, beginning and ending with flour. Put a very thin layer of batter —about 7 tablespoons—in each pan, shaking the pans to distribute the batter to the edges. Bake the layers for 11 to 13 minutes. Remove the layers from the pans and frost immediately with the warm icing. Bake all of the remaining batter in this manner, building layers. You should be able to get 12 layers from this recipe.

If the idea of all these layers is too much for you, divide the batter evenly into three cake pans. It tastes great, no matter how many layers you make.

pumpkin roll

From Thanksgiving through Christmas, I'm in heaven because I get to make all of my signature dishes for my family and friends. It's always special when a friend drops by to bring something he or she has made for you. It's really one of the sweetest gifts someone can give you, because the person has put his or her love and time into it. Every year, my friend Kim makes the Pumpkin Roll for her Thanksgiving table, and she always bakes an extra one for me. It makes our family gathering all the more special. **SERVES 16**

3 large eggs

1 cup granulated sugar

⅔ cup canned pumpkin

1 teaspoon lemon juice

¾ cup all-purpose flour

1 teaspoon ground ginger

½ teaspoon salt

1 teaspoon baking powder

2 teaspoons ground cinnamon

1 cup pecans, finely chopped

1 cup confectioners' sugar, plus more for sprinkling

2 3-ounce packages cream cheese, room temperature

½ cup (1 stick) butter, room temperature

½ teaspoon vanilla extract

Preheat the oven to 350°F. Grease and flour a 17½ × 12½-inch jellyroll pan. (Jellyroll pan sizes may vary.)

With an electric mixer, beat the eggs, sugar, pumpkin, and lemon juice until smooth. Sift together the flour, ginger, salt, baking powder, and cinnamon. Add to the mixer and blend until fully combined. Spread the batter in the jellyroll pan. Sprinkle the dough with the chopped pecans. Bake for 14 minutes, or until a cake tester inserted in the center comes out clean. Let the cake cool in the pan for 5 minutes.

Invert the cake onto a wire rack lined with parchment paper and let it cool completely. Sprinkle some of the confectioners' sugar on a large tea towel and transfer the cake to the towel. Roll the cake up in the towel and cool in the refrigerator thoroughly, about 45 minutes.

With an electric mixer, combine the 1 cup confectioners' sugar, the cream cheese, butter, and vanilla and beat until smooth. Unroll the cooled cake and spread the mixture on top of the cake. Gently roll the cake up and refrigerate it until you're ready to slice and serve. Dust with confectioners' sugar just before serving.

chocolate pie

This recipe comes from family friend Mack Tillman. Mr. Mack was a tall drink of water, like my daddy. He was the Jasper County sheriff, and later he opened what I think is the best restaurant in Georgia, the Tillman House. After Mr. Mack passed away, the restaurant was kept in the family and run by his son and daughter, Ben and Sissy. We all lived on Eatonton Street in Monticello when I was a little girl, and Sissy and I were best buddies. Mr. Mack made the best fried chicken I have ever tasted (sorry, Mama!) and this amazing chocolate pie. Most people use a 9-inch prebaked pastry shell, but I make it with a graham cracker crust. **SERVES 8**

CRUST

1½ cups fine graham cracker crumbs

¼ cup sugar

¼ cup (½ stick) butter, melted

FILLING

1 cup sugar

1 tablespoon unsweetened cocoa powder

3 tablespoons self-rising flour

3 large eggs, separated

1 cup milk

2 tablespoons butter, melted

½ teaspoon vanilla extract

Pinch of salt

In a mixing bowl, stir together the graham cracker crumbs, sugar, and butter until the crumbs are coated. Press the mixture firmly into the bottom of a 9-inch pie plate. Set aside.

In the top of a double boiler, mix the sugar, cocoa, and flour. Lightly beat the egg yolks (save the whites for the meringue) and stir in the milk. Slowly add the egg-milk mixture to the sugar mixture in the double boiler, creating a paste in the beginning; this will ensure that the chocolate and flour blend smoothly. Cook in the double boiler until very thick, 45 to 50 minutes. When the spoon is moved in the filling, it will leave a brief indention or trough. Remove the boiler from the heat and stir in the melted butter, the vanilla, and the salt. Stir well to mix in the butter.

Pour the filling into the crust. Allow the pie to cool in the refrigerator for 45 minutes before putting a meringue on top.

recipe continues

SEP • 67

My best pals! *From left to right:* Beth, me, Sissy, Paula Lane, Ben, and Sydney Lane.
Sydney's dog, Toby, is in the back row.

MERINGUE
3 large egg whites
Pinch of salt
5 tablespoons sugar

To prepare the meringue, preheat the oven to 325°F. With an electric mixer, beat the egg whites with the salt until stiff. Add the sugar gradually as you continue beating until the whites are smooth and glossy. Spread the meringue over the pie, all the way to touch and seal the edges of the crust. Bake for 15 to 20 minutes, until brown. Cool completely before serving.

Instead of using a meringue, you could sprinkle the top of the pie liberally with graham cracker crumbs.

magic lemon meringue pie

I ate this pie a lot while I was growing up in Georgia, and I never knew who had the recipe. Turns out my mama had it all along! Edward's Pies makes a really good frozen lemon meringue pie, but I can't find it out here in Oklahoma. Edward's products date back to the 1950s, and if you ever have one, be sure to check the box for a Bible verse. They're known for that, and I guess that makes me like them even more, because I always include a Bible verse on my CDs. I made this homemade version of the pie for the first time recently. When I realized that I could actually make this myself and enjoy it whenever I wanted, I was thrilled. Garth isn't a big fan of meringue, so sometimes I double the filling for this pie and leave off the meringue. That's double the magic! Thanks for the inspiration, Edward's. SERVES 10

CRUST
1½ cups fine graham cracker crumbs

¼ cup sugar

¼ cup (½ stick) butter, melted

FILLING
1 14-ounce can sweetened condensed milk

½ cup fresh lemon juice (about 2 large lemons)

1 teaspoon grated lemon zest

3 large egg yolks, whites reserved for meringue

MERINGUE
3 large egg whites

¼ teaspoon cream of tartar

¼ cup sugar

Preheat the oven to 325°F.

In a mixing bowl, stir together the graham cracker crumbs, sugar, and butter until fully combined. Press the mixture firmly into a 9-inch pie plate. Set aside.

In a medium bowl, mix the condensed milk, lemon juice, zest, and egg yolks. Pour the mixture into the crust.

Beat the egg whites and cream of tartar in a medium bowl with an electric hand mixer until soft peaks form. Gradually beat in the sugar until stiff peaks form.

Spread the meringue over the pie and seal to the edge of the crust. Bake for 15 to 20 minutes, or until the meringue browns slightly. Chill for at least 2 hours before serving.

FROM GWEN: Be sure to watch the pie while it's baking. Meringue can burn quickly.

cookies, candy, etc.

I tell people who are afraid to cook because they think it's too hard to start with something simple, like baking cookies. It's a good way to get your culinary feet wet, and it's fun. My experience has taught me that even a cookie that turns out badly is usually good! Once you get the hang of it, you might move to the hard stuff, like Mama's Never-Fail Divinity (page 212).

We're all called upon from time to time to take something to a bake sale or fund-raiser. The next time you're asked, before you are tempted to buy a box of cookies from the grocery store, try one of these recipes. Surprise yourself and your friends!

jennifer's iced sugar cookies

When Beth lived in west Tennessee, she began a tradition of baking cookies with friends during the Christmas holidays. At their first cookie baking, Jennifer Vincent shared this recipe for rolled sugar cookies, letting the children roll, cut, and decorate them. Even though Beth and her family have moved back to Georgia, they have continued the tradition with their new friends, and even though many of the children are all grown up, they still make these cookies at their annual Christmas cookie party. Everybody doubles the dough so they'll have plenty to decorate and share. Her tradition has spilled over to Oklahoma. **MAKES 15 TO 17 MEDIUM COOKIES**

COOKIES

2 cups all-purpose flour

2 teaspoons baking powder

½ teaspoon salt

½ cup (1 stick) butter

1 cup granulated sugar

1 large egg

½ teaspoon vanilla extract

ICING

1 1-pound box confectioners' sugar

3 tablespoons meringue powder (see Note)

⅓ cup warm (80–90° F) water

Food coloring (optional)

Assorted sprinkles, colored sugar, and small candy pieces

Sift together the flour, baking powder, and salt. In a large mixing bowl, cream the butter and sugar until light and fluffy. Add the egg and mix until combined. Gradually add the sifted dry ingredients, one spoonful at a time, until thoroughly combined. Add the vanilla. Chill the cookie dough in the refrigerator for at least 1 hour.

Preheat the oven to 400°F. Roll out half of the dough at a time, keeping the remainder of the dough in the refrigerator. On a lightly floured surface, roll out the dough to a ¼-inch thickness and cut it into desired shapes with a cookie cutter. Place the cutout cookies 2 inches apart on an ungreased cookie sheet and put the cookie sheet in the refrigerator for a few minutes before baking. This will help the cookies retain their shape. (You can roll out the scraps to make a few more cookies.) Bake for 8 to 10 minutes, or until just before the edges of the cookies start to brown. Cool the cookies for 1 to 2 minutes on the cookie sheet before removing to wire racks to cool completely.

NOTE: Meringue powder is available in a can. (I use Wilton.) It is used in place of egg whites in many icing recipes.

In a medium bowl, combine the confectioners' sugar, meringue powder, and warm water with a wire whisk. Stir until the icing is smooth. Adjust the consistency of the icing by adding more confectioners' sugar or more water, as needed. Add food coloring, if desired, to the icing. Spread the icing on the cooled cookies and then top with assorted sprinkles and candies.

Counterclockwise from bottom left: Jennifer's Iced Sugar Cookies, Lizzie's Chocolate Pinwheel Cookies, Venita's Chocolate Chip Cookies, Mamie's Teacakes, Lemon Squares, and Thumbprint Cookies.

thumbprint cookies

These cookies are always on the baking list at Beth's annual Christmas cookie party. Cream cheese and almond flavoring in the dough make these nut-covered cookies extra special. And for the "icing on the cake," you fill the "thumbprints" with the icing from Jennifer's Iced Sugar Cookies (page 190)! **MAKES 2 DOZEN COOKIES**

1 cup vegetable shortening, such as Crisco

1 3-ounce package cream cheese, room temperature

1 cup sugar

1 large egg

1 teaspoon almond extract

2½ cups all-purpose flour

¼ teaspoon baking soda

½ teaspoon salt

1¼ cups finely chopped pecans

Icing from Jennifer's Iced Sugar Cookies (page 190)

In the bowl of an electric mixer, cream the shortening, cream cheese, and sugar until smooth. Add the egg and almond extract. Sift together the flour, baking soda, and salt, and stir into the shortening mixture. When thoroughly mixed, chill the dough in the refrigerator for 1 hour.

Preheat the oven to 350°F. Shape the dough into 1½-inch balls, roll the balls in the chopped pecans, and place on an ungreased cookie sheet. Bake for 12 to 15 minutes, or until lightly browned. Remove the baked cookies from the oven while still warm, and use your finger or a wooden spoon handle to make a "thumb-print" in the center of each cookie. Fill the indentation with the icing. Transfer the cookies to wire racks for cooling.

Fill these cookies with your favorite jelly or jam for a different flavor.

> FROM BETH: Ask your children to make the actual "thumbprints" in the cookies.

lizzie's chocolate pinwheel cookies

Grandma Lizzie made these little cookies that looked like they could spin. They're not only pretty but also delicious. Grandma would always have some sort of sweet treat baking when we arrived for a visit. These pinwheels were as fun to play with as they were to eat. **MAKES 2 DOZEN COOKIES**

½ cup vegetable shortening, such as Crisco

½ cup sugar

1 large egg yolk

1½ teaspoons vanilla extract

1½ cups all-purpose flour

½ teaspoon baking powder

¼ teaspoon salt

3 tablespoons milk

1 ounce (1 square) unsweetened baking chocolate, melted

NOTE: When cutting the roll, use a very sharp knife and wipe the blade after each slice to avoid mixing the colors and to keep the cookies round. You could also use an electric knife.

Cream the shortening and sugar. Add the egg yolk and vanilla. Mix well.

Sift the flour with the baking powder and salt. Add the flour mixture and milk alternately to the shortening mixture, beginning and ending with the flour. Divide the dough into two halves. To one half, add the chocolate, mixing thoroughly. Wrap both sections of dough in separate pieces of plastic wrap and chill in the refrigerator for about 1 hour.

Unwrap and roll each half of dough between 2 pieces of waxed paper. Roll to a ⅛-inch thickness. Remove the waxed paper from the top of each layer of dough. Place the white layer on top of the chocolate layer, and roll up carefully as you would a jellyroll, using the waxed paper to roll smoothly. Wrap the roll with the waxed paper and chill overnight in the refrigerator.

The next day, preheat the oven to 375°F. Cut the roll into ¼-inch slices (see Note) and place about ½ inch apart on an ungreased cookie sheet. Bake for about 12 minutes. Do not brown. Remove carefully with a pancake turner and cool on racks.

To cut the dough with a thread, slide a 12-inch length under the roll, cross it over at the top, and pull right through.

fruitcake cookies

I'm not a fan of fruitcake, but these Fruitcake Cookies are delicious and are a special favorite of my sister, Beth. The ladies of Shady Dale, Georgia—among them, Mrs. Fannie Newton (the grandmother of my high school friend Lynn Newton Deraney) and Mrs. Sara Martin—were known as great cooks. They made and sold baked goods to places as far away as King Plow Company in Atlanta, Georgia. For this reason, some of their recipes were closely guarded secrets. However, they were very generous in sharing the baked goods locally. (We're told that Miss Sara didn't cook but was the delivery person!) They would send goodies to the Bank of Monticello, where Daddy worked and, somehow, he managed to get a copy of this recipe. I'm sure it was his southern gentleman's charm.

MAKES 14½ DOZEN COOKIES

3 cups all-purpose flour

1 teaspoon baking soda

1 teaspoon ground cinnamon

1 cup light brown sugar, packed

1 cup (2 sticks) butter, room temperature

3 large eggs, lightly beaten

½ cup whole milk

7 cups coarsely chopped pecans (about 2 pounds whole pecans)

2 cups candied cherries, chopped

6 slices candied pineapple, chopped

1 15-ounce box golden raisins, chopped

Preheat the oven to 300°F. Grease a cookie sheet.

Sift together the flour, baking soda, and cinnamon. Cream the butter and sugar, then gradually add the eggs. Add the dry ingredients alternately with the milk, blending well. Mix the fruits and pecans in a large bowl, then pour the batter over them. Fold the fruit into the batter by hand, mixing well. Drop the batter by teaspoonfuls onto the cookie sheet. Bake for 20 to 25 minutes, or until done.

Daddy always said this recipe made a blue million. That's a lot, for those of you who are wondering!

From left to right: "Miss" Fannie Newton, Lynn Newton Deraney, and "Miss" Sara Martin.

venita's chocolate chip cookies

Everyone has a favorite chocolate chip cookie recipe, but this one just might replace yours! This is *the* signature cookie for Beth's friend Venita. It takes a little extra time to blend oatmeal and grate chocolate bars, but trust me—it's worth it! These cookies are a staple for family gatherings, college care packages, and beach potlucks.

MAKES 6 DOZEN COOKIES

¾ cup (1½ sticks) butter, room temperature

¼ cup vegetable shortening, such as Crisco

1 cup granulated sugar

1 cup light brown sugar

2 large eggs

1 teaspoon vanilla extract

2½ cups old-fashioned rolled oats

2 cups all-purpose flour

½ teaspoon salt

1 teaspoon baking powder

1 teaspoon baking soda

6 ounces semisweet chocolate chips (about 1 cup)

1 5-ounce Hershey's chocolate bar, grated or chopped

1½ cups chopped pecans (optional)

Preheat the oven to 400°F.

With an electric mixer, cream the butter, shortening, and sugars until smooth. Add the eggs and vanilla, mixing well. In a blender or food processor, process the oats to a fine powder. Sift together the flour, salt, baking powder, baking soda, and oatmeal and, with the mixer running, gradually add to the creamed mixture. Stir in the chocolate chips, grated chocolate bar, and pecans, if using.

Roll the dough into golf-size balls and place 2 inches apart on an ungreased cookie sheet. Bake for 7 to 8 minutes. With a spatula, loosen the baked cookies from the pan and allow them to cool on the cookie sheet. Serve warm.

mamie's teacakes

My parents' first apartment was in a lovely old home in Monticello, Georgia, owned by the town librarian, Miss Mary Murrelle. When my folks built their first house, it was just down the street and "Mamie," as we called Miss Mary, had become a lifelong friend. She made the best teacakes, which were soft and had a cakelike texture. My mom, sister, and I have collected recipes for years trying to replicate that teacake. These come close! Just make sure you don't overwork the dough. The less you work the dough, the lighter and fluffier the cookie. **MAKES 3 DOZEN TEACAKES**

3½ cups all-purpose flour
1 teaspoon baking soda
¼ teaspoon salt
½ cup (1 stick) butter, room temperature
1½ cups sugar
2 large eggs
1½ teaspoons vanilla extract
¼ cup sour cream

Preheat the oven to 400°F. Grease 2 large (14 × 16-inch) cookie sheets with solid shortening.

Sift together the flour, baking soda, and salt. Using an electric mixer on medium speed, combine the butter, sugar, eggs, and vanilla. Add the sour cream and mix well. On low speed, gradually add the flour mixture until well blended. Turn the dough out onto a lightly floured board, and pat with floured hands to a ¼-inch thickness. Cut with a 2-inch round, floured cookie cutter and place on cookie sheets about 1 inch apart. Bake for 10 to 12 minutes, until the teacakes are lightly browned. Do not overbake. Using an egg turner, remove the cookies to a rack to cool.

The dough is sticky, but be careful about adding too much extra flour when shaping the teacakes. By using care, patience, and a floured egg turner when patting and cutting, you will be rewarded with tasty, tender teacakes.

vicki's shortbread

This past Christmas, we came home from Christmas Eve church service to find a pan of this shortbread sitting on the steps. Thank goodness Beth's cat Ferrari (don't ask) is 100 years old and has long ago lost her sense of smell. We devoured the shortbread in short order (I know, pun intended). "I'll bet Vicki Walker brought this by," Beth said. By the way, Vicki, I'll be at my sister's house again this Christmas . . . I'm just sayin'. SERVES 16

1 cup self-rising flour

½ cup (1 stick) butter, room temperature

¼ cup granulated sugar

¼ cup brown sugar

Preheat the oven to 350°F. Spray a 9-inch pie pan with cooking spray.

With an electric mixer, mix the flour, butter, and sugars together until fully combined. Spread the mixture in the bottom of the pie pan. Bake for 25 minutes. Cool and slice.

A slice of shortbread with a hot cup of coffee is one of my favorite afternoon snacks during the holidays.

grape salad

This is a popular salad in Georgia. A family friend, Bobbie Jean Ozburn, first took it to a Monticello Woman's Club luncheon and it became known as "That Woman's Club Grape Salad." There are a lot of versions of this salad out there. It's called a salad, but it's really more of a dessert. **SERVES 12**

2 pounds seedless green grapes

2 pounds seedless purple grapes

1 8-ounce package cream cheese, room temperature

1 8-ounce container sour cream

½ cup granulated sugar

1 teaspoon vanilla extract

1 cup brown sugar, firmly packed

1 cup pecans, finely chopped

Wash the grapes and dry thoroughly with paper towels. Put the dry grapes in a large bowl. In a separate bowl, stir the cream cheese until it is smooth. Add the sour cream, granulated sugar, and vanilla. Mix well. Pour this mixture over the grapes and toss together until all grapes are coated. Pour the grapes into a 9 × 12-inch pan. Refrigerate overnight.

Just before serving, sprinkle with the brown sugar and pecans.

lemon squares

This is the first thing I ever made that had confectioners' sugar in the crust. I could eat this crust all by itself! Our youngest daughter, Allie Colleen, is the aspiring cook in our family, and this is one of her specialties. MAKES 15 SQUARES

CRUST

1 cup (2 sticks) butter, room temperature

2 cups all-purpose flour

½ cup confectioners' sugar

FILLING

4 large eggs

5 tablespoons fresh lemon juice (from about 2 large lemons)

2 tablespoons grated lemon zest

2 cups granulated sugar

1 tablespoon all-purpose flour

1 teaspoon baking powder

½ teaspoon salt

Confectioners' sugar, for sprinkling

Preheat the oven to 350°F. Spray a 9 × 13 × 2-inch pan with cooking spray.

In a medium saucepan, melt the butter. Remove from the heat and add the flour and confectioners' sugar, mixing until a dough forms. Press the mixture firmly into the pan. Bake the crust for 25 minutes.

While the crust is baking, with an electric mixer, combine the eggs, lemon juice, and zest until smooth. Add the granulated sugar, flour, baking powder, and salt, and beat until smooth. Pour the mixture over the baked crust. Bake for 25 minutes more. Remove the pan from the oven and let it cool completely. Sprinkle the top with confectioners' sugar. Cut into squares and serve.

bess london's pecan tassies

Bess London is a friend of mine. Garth and I have known her son Emmett for years, and when I moved to Oklahoma, she was one of the first people I met. She's in her nineties and still as active and lively as ever. She is a true inspiration and the kind of woman I want to be. She raised three boys in rural Mississippi and has so many great stories about them. Even though they are grown men now, Bess can still embarrass them with a good story from childhood. She is also an amazing cook, and believes, like me, that one way you can show people you love them is to cook for them. The first treats Miss Bess ever made for me were these Pecan Tassies. I have to say that, even following her recipe to the letter, I find that hers are lighter and tastier than mine. It must be all of that love! MAKES 24 TASSIES

½ cup (1 stick) butter, room temperature, plus 1 tablespoon butter, melted

1 3-ounce package cream cheese, room temperature

1 cup all-purpose flour

1 large egg

¾ cup packed light brown sugar

1 teaspoon vanilla extract

Pinch of salt

½ cup pecans, finely chopped

With an electric mixer, beat the ½ cup butter and the cream cheese until smooth. Add the flour and beat until fully combined. Cover the bowl with plastic wrap and chill in the refrigerator for 1 hour.

Preheat the oven to 325°F. Spray a mini-muffin pan with cooking spray.

In a large mixing bowl, whisk together the melted butter, egg, brown sugar, vanilla, and salt until smooth. Set aside.

Shape the chilled dough into 24 balls, about 1 inch in diameter. Press each ball into a cup of the muffin pan, then spoon 1 teaspoon of the pecans into each muffin cup. Fill each cup with the egg mixture until evenly distributed. Bake for 25 minutes, or until the filling is set. Cool on a wire rack for 10 minutes, then remove from the muffin pan.

Garth and Miss Bess at our wedding, December 10, 2005.

betty's apple ambrosia

In my family, ambrosia is usually made with oranges, coconut, and sugar. My friend Betty Maxwell used to make this for my daddy all the time. He loved ambrosia. You don't have to wait until oranges are in the peak season to enjoy this—just use a lot more sugar for sweetness. MAKES 6 CUPS

1 cup orange juice with lots of pulp, or more as needed

3 ripe Delicious apples

1 8-ounce can crushed pineapple

¼ cup sugar

½ cup frozen grated coconut, thawed

Pour the orange juice into a medium bowl. Peel and core the apples, then grate them into the orange juice using the large-hole side of the grater. Add the pineapple, sugar, and coconut. Mix well, adding more orange juice if the mixture is not juicy enough. The apples will continue to absorb juice, and orange juice can be added as needed to keep it as juicy as you like. Store in the refrigerator until ready to serve.

Choose a sweet apple that you like. My favorite is Golden Delicious.

crockpot chocolate candy

My cousin Donna Paulk is a great cook. She's kindly given us several great recipes for this collection, including chicken soup, macaroni and cheese, beignets, and this candy. I love this kind of recipe: the candies look so pretty and appear really hard to make. People will think you're a genius cook, which is almost embarrassing considering how easy they are to make. Just layer everything in the cooker and wait! **MAKES 30 TO 40 PIECES**

2 pounds (36 ounces) salted dry-roasted peanuts

4 ounces (4 squares) German's sweet chocolate

1 12-ounce package semisweet chocolate chips (about 2 cups)

2½ pounds white almond bark

FROM BETH: This is a fun recipe to make with your children. They can put everything in the slow cooker, and drop the candy into the cupcake liners, too.

Put the peanuts in the bottom of a 4-quart slow cooker. Layer the chocolate over the peanuts, beginning with the sweet chocolate, followed by the chocolate chips, and then the almond bark. Set the temperature on low and cook for 3 hours. Do not stir the mixture.

After 3 hours, stir the mixture with a wooden spoon until smooth. Drop the candy into cupcake pan liners using about 2 tablespoons per liner. Allow the candy to cool completely before removing the cupcake liners.

If you can't find almond bark, substitute white chocolate chips.

"miss" mickey's peanut butter balls

One summer our friends Patty and Pam were having a garage sale. Our girls Taylor and August wanted to have a lemonade stand, so they made a sign to hang on the front of their card table, and they set up shop during the garage sale. Patty and Pam's sweet neighbor Howard saw the girls and came over to buy some lemonade. Shortly after that, Howard's wife, Mickey, came over with some cookies and some peanut butter balls to give the girls. After that day, any time the girls were visiting Patty and Pam, they'd go see Howard and "Miss" Mickey. Mickey passed away several years ago, but Howard is eighty-one and still going strong. Garth and the girls make these peanut butter balls to give as gifts, and they always remember "Miss" Mickey when they make them. MAKES ABOUT 40 BALLS

1 cup sugar
½ cup dark corn syrup
½ cup white corn syrup
2 cups crunchy peanut butter
4 cups Rice Krispies

In a large saucepan, stir the sugar and the syrups together over medium heat. Add the peanut butter and continue to stir until the mixture is fully combined. Remove the pan from the heat, and add the Rice Krispies. Mix well. Spray your hands lightly with cooking spray and shape the mixture into balls. Transfer to waxed paper. Store in an airtight container for up to 2 weeks.

August and Taylor and their lemonade stand.

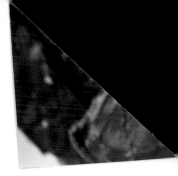

peanut butter bars

These peanut butter bars came from Beth's sister-in-law, Margaret Ann Akins. She says her daughter Amanda requests them for her birthday instead of cake. Mama and Beth spent a weekend testing all kinds of brownies and bars, and they sent some to school with Beth's children on Monday morning. When my mom drove the carpool that afternoon, she overheard my nine-year-old nephew, Bret, and his friends in the backseat discussing the cookbook. Bret spoke up and said to her, "Grammy, we have another two thumbs up for the Peanut Butter Bars!" If a nine-year-old says they're good, what more do you need to know? They're perfect for a picnic or a day at the lake. **MAKES 3 DOZEN 1 X 3-INCH BARS**

½ cup (1 stick) butter, room temperature

½ cup granulated sugar

½ cup packed brown sugar

½ cup plus 4 tablespoons creamy peanut butter

1 large egg, beaten

1 teaspoon vanilla extract

1 cup all-purpose flour

1 teaspoon baking soda

¼ teaspoon salt

½ cup quick-cooking oatmeal

6 ounces semisweet chocolate chips (about 1 cup)

1 cup confectioners' sugar

4 tablespoons milk

Preheat the oven to 350°F. Grease a 9 × 13 × 2-inch baking dish.

Using an electric mixer, cream the butter, sugars, and ½ cup peanut butter. Add the egg and vanilla. Sift the flour with the baking soda and the salt. Mix the oatmeal into the flour and stir the flour into the creamed mixture. Spread the batter in the baking pan. Sprinkle the chocolate chips over the batter and bake for 20 to 25 minutes, until browned around the edges.

Mix the confectioners' sugar, remaining 4 tablespoons peanut butter, and milk. Blend until smooth, then spread over the warm Peanut Butter Bars.

sweet and saltines

After a meal, my mama will always say, "I need a little something sweet." If she has dessert, she will inevitably follow it up with, "Now I need a little something salty." It's become a joke at our house. These crackers are so good, you will just keep eating them, and Mama has her sweet and salty thing covered. Beware, they're really addictive.

SERVES 20

40 saltine crackers

1 cup (2 sticks) butter

1 cup light brown sugar

8 ounces semisweet chocolate chips (about 1⅓ cups)

Preheat the oven to 425°F. Line a large jellyroll pan with aluminum foil and the saltine crackers.

In a medium saucepan, melt the butter and brown sugar together and bring to a boil. Boil for 5 minutes. Remove from the heat and pour over the crackers, covering them evenly. Put the jellyroll pan into the oven and watch closely. Bake for 4 to 5 minutes, or until just bubbly. Remove from the oven and pour the chocolate chips over the crackers. When the chips melt a bit, spread them over the crackers with a knife. Transfer the pan to the freezer for 15 to 20 minutes, or until completely cold. They will form one big sheet. Break up into pieces. Store in an airtight container.

FROM GWEN: Use anywhere from 35 to 45 saltine crackers, depending on the size of your pan.

FROM BETH: I used milk chocolate chips instead of semisweet once because that's what I had on hand. They tasted great, too.

Substitute graham crackers for the saltines for a sweeter snack. Use 1 stick of butter instead of 2 for a crunchier, saltier cracker.

never-fail divinity

This is another family favorite of mine from childhood. I always thought these perfect white candy pieces looked so elegant. They are really rich, so you shouldn't eat too many at a time! My mom makes this recipe, and my only rule is "Always eat divinity when it's in the house, rain or shine!" **MAKES ABOUT 2 DOZEN CANDIES**

2 cups sugar

½ cup cold water

½ cup light corn syrup

Pinch of salt

2 large egg whites, stiffly beaten

1 teaspoon vanilla extract

1 cup chopped pecans or walnuts

In a large saucepan, stir the sugar, water, syrup, and salt together until the sugar dissolves. Cook on medium heat to 260°F, or until the mixture spins a long thread. Pour one third of the boiling syrup over the beaten egg whites, beating continuously. Add the vanilla. Cook the remaining syrup over medium heat until it reaches the hard boil stage, 300°F. Pour this syrup over the egg-white mixture and continue beating until the candy holds a soft shape. Stir in the nuts and drop by teaspoonfuls on waxed paper or pour into an 8 × 8 × 2-inch pan. Allow the candy to harden.

FROM BETH: Double beaters are a must when making this candy.

FROM MAMA: Dorothy Cliett, from Grandma Lizzie's side of the family, cooks the syrup twice to ensure that the candy will be firm.

thanks

I'll never be able to thank everyone who helped make this second collaboration possible! So many people rose to the occasion to make this cookbook come alive. Thanks to everyone at Clarkson Potter, especially Emily Takoudes for tackling the editing job on the heels of having a new baby! Thank you to Jenny Beal Davis for designing a beautiful book . . . again! Thanks to Lauren Shakely, Doris Cooper, Kate Tyler, and Peggy Paul. Special thanks to Ken Levitan, Michelle Owens, and Vector Management for continuing to bring me fun opportunities like this one.

When something works the first time, you stick with it. Ben Fink, your talents continue to amaze me. Thank you for photographing our food and for taking such care to make sure it was absolutely perfect. Special thanks to Jeff Kavanaugh, Jamie Kimm, Barb Fritz, Ruby Guidara, and Cynthia Winn for photographing, styling, and preparing everything necessary for the photo shoots in New York and Nashville. Thank you to Russ Harrington for shooting the cover and to Eli McFadden,

Joel Hood, and Brent Harrington for assisting. Thanks to Matt Harrington and Luellyn Latocki for PhotoShop Botox! Sorry about the mosquitos! Thank you Bev Parker for capturing the love I feel for my cowboy.

Thanks to the crew in Nashville: Gary Birdwell, Lark Foster, Steve Gibson, Tracy Greenwood, Jarrah Herter, Terri McGee, and Steve McLellan. You made it all work! Thank you, Hope Baldwin, for driving down to Willacoochee, Georgia, to take pictures at the Paulk family reunion. The crockpot mac and cheese is in the mail! Melissa Perry, thanks for coming to the party a second time and preparing all of these recipes. I think your being seven months pregnant during this process made you enjoy the food even more! Thanks to Earl Cox, Mary Beth Felts, Claudia Fowler, and Amanda Kaye West, for hair, makeup, and wardrobe for all of the Yearwood women!

Thank you to the family and friends who contributed recipes and photos for this cookbook. You all really came through for us! Thank you for your love and generosity:

Faye Abercrombie, Louise Aiken, Margaret Akins, Betty Alexander, Frank and Loretta Bruce, Linda Buchanan, Charlene Burton, Larue Camp, Colleen Cates, Nellie Chaires, Lydia Clements, Melba Clements, Dorothy Cliett, Mandy Smith Corley, Elizabeth Davis, Shirley Davis, Lynn Deraney, Shirley Durden, Pat Foster, Paula Funderburke, Shirley Anne Gilliam, Cordelia Goodman, Rita Goodman, Clarice Hamby, Lynn Hamby, Mary Cam Harding, Sissy Hayes, Pam Helm, Patti Helm, Nancy Hinds, Sissy Tillman Hulsey, Geraldine Johnson, Mary Lou Jordan, Iris Kicklighter, Diane Knight, Hope Kozma, Sydney Lane, Peggy Leach, Cynthia Lee, Kim

LeFlore, Bess London, Leona Lucine, Vicki Martin, Pat McCormack, Ruth McCormick, Joann Mosley, Karen Oakes, Bobbie Jean Ozburn, Donna Paulk, Emily Paulk, Fred and Dorothy Sue Paulk, Michele Paulk, Warren and Linda Paulk, Wilson and Beth Paulk, Julianne Perry, Phyllis Pritchett, Amanda Richey, Jodi Roberts, Lindsey Rundorff, Terry Rundorff, Kate Sandifer, Mark and Venita Sandifer, Kathryn Sauls, Gail Sealy, Mae Sears, Gail Shoup, Medea Shuman, Donna Smith, Eryn Smith, Stan and Mari Smith, Vicki Smith, Angela Spivey, Tricia Stafford, Howard Stamper, Angela Stewart, Mandy Stewart, Brian and Becky Tankersley, Lynne Tanner, Ben Tillman, Aletha Tyler, Sandy Vandegrift, Jennifer Vincent, Chrystal Vining, Vicki Walker, Margaret Watson, Tana Weber, Amanda Paulk Wildes, Nona Wilson, Susan Winslett, Stone Workman, Dianne Yearwood, Pete Yearwood, and SuSan Yearwood.

A huge thank-you to our immediate families, John, Ashley, Kyle, and Bret Bernard and Garth, Taylor, August, and Allie Brooks: Thank you for trying anything we put on the table and for being patient while we spent hours in front of the computer. We love you all.

Finally, thank you to Mama (Gwen) and Beth, for taking this journey with me again. You cooked, tested, counseled, laughed, and cried with me! I am so lucky you're my family. I love you.

index

Page references in *italic* refer to illustrations.

aiken, Louise, 53
Akins, Margaret Ann, 209
almond(s):
    bark, in Crockpot Chocolate
        Candy, 206, *207*
    Chicken and Wild Rice Casserole,
        106, 107
    Chicken Poppy Seed Salad, 76,
        77
    Strawberry Salad, 68, *69*
Ambrosia, Apple, Betty's, *204*, 205
American cheese, in Rainy Day
    Chicken and Rice Soup, 62
appetizers, *see* snacks and appetizers
apple(s):
    Ambrosia, Betty's, *204*, 205
    Dumplings, 30, *31*
    Fresh, Cake, *156*, 157
    Red Candy, *56*, 57
Asparagus Bundles, *126*, 127

bacon:
    adding to waffles, 20
    Asparagus Bundles, *126*, 127
    Breakfast Bowl, Garth's, *24*, 25
    Charleston Cheese Dip, *44*, 45
    Chicken Bites, Warren's, 50, *50*
    Cornbread Salad with French
        Dressing, *70*, 71
    Potato Casserole, 132
    Twice-Baked Potatoes, *128*, *129*
Baked Bean Casserole, 133
Barbecued Pork Ribs, Fred's, *96*, 97
Bass, Saucy, 108
bean(s):
    Baked, Casserole, 133
    black, in Fancy Chili, 64, *65*
    black, in Tennessee Jambalaya, 63
Beater Blade, 15
beef, 81–89

Baked Bean Casserole, 133
Baked Spaghetti, *86*, 87
Cabbage Rolls, Colleen's, 84, *85*
corned, in Cheese Boat, 48
Cowboy Lasagne, *92*, 93
Fancy Chili, 64, *65*
Meatballs, 91
Roast, Cordelia's, 88, *89*
Roast, Hash, 88
Stuffed Bell Peppers, Uncle
    Wilson's, *82*, 83
Beignets, *36*, 37
Bernard, Ashley, 33
Bernard, Beth Yearwood, 19, 34, 37,
    61, 64, 68, 93, 101, 105, 109, 110,
    116, 120, 142, 145, 150, 153, 161,
    172, 177, 178, 190, 192, 206, 209,
    211, 212
Bernard, Blanche, 153
Bernard, Bret, 30, 153, 172, 209
Bernard, John, 153
Bernard, Kyle, 22, 134
Bess London's Pecan Tassies, 202,
    203
Betty's Apple Ambrosia, *204*, 205
biscuits:
    buttermilk canned, in Apple
        Dumplings, 30, *31*
    canned, in Monkey Bread Muffins,
        32, 33
    drop: Easiest Muffins, *140*, 141
    Old-Fashioned Strawberry Short-
        cake, 164, *165*
black beans:
    Fancy Chili, 64, *65*
    Tennessee Jambalaya, 63
Blanche's Miniature Cherry Muffins,
    153
Blueberry Pancakes, 22, *23*
Blue Cheese Dressing, *66*, 67
bread(s), 139–53
    Broccoli Cornbread, 150, *151*
    Cheese Boat, 48
    Cherry Muffins, Miniature,
        Blanche's, 153

Cranberry, *146*, 147
Jalapeño Hushpuppies, 152
Monkey, 33
Monkey, Muffins, *32*, 33
Muffins, Easiest, *140*, 141
Pumpkin, Pat's, 148
Raisin, Margaret's, 145
Sour Cream Cornbread, 144
Spoon Rolls, 142, *143*
Zucchini, 149
breakfast, 17–37
    Apple Dumplings, 30, *31*
    Beignets, *36*, 37
    Blueberry Pancakes, 22, *23*
    Bowl, Garth's, *24*, 25
    Cinnamon Rolls, 34, *35*
    Country Quiche, 26, *27*
    Hawaiian Fresh Fruit Salad, 28, *29*
    Monkey Bread Muffins, *32*, 33
    for supper, 22
    Waffles with Hot Maple Syrup,
        Mama's Homemade, *18*, 19–20,
        21
broccoli:
    Casserole, *118*, 119
    Cornbread, 150, *151*
Brooks, Allie Colleen, 201
Brooks, August, 155, 208
Brooks, Colleen, 84
Brooks, Garth, 9, 25, 26, 84, 120, 187,
    202, 208
Brooks, Taylor, 208
Bruce, Marie Yearwood, 163
bundt cakes:
    Fresh Apple, *156*, 157
    greasing pans for, 15, 157
    Buttermilk Glaze, *156*, 157

Cabbage:
    Casserole, *130*, 131
    Crunchy Slaw, 116, *117*
    Rolls, Colleen's, 84, *85*
    Thai Salad, Ty's, 72, 73
Cake Release (Wilton), 15, 178

cakes, 155–81
  Apple, Fresh, *156*, 157
  Carrot, *166*, 167–68
  Chocolate, with Divinity Icing, *174*, 175–76
  Chocolate Torte, 177–78, *179*
  Coconut, with Coconut Lemon Glaze, Grandma Yearwood's, 169
  icing, tools for, 15
  Key Lime, *160*, 161–62
  Pound, Cold-Oven, 163
  Pumpkin Roll, *180*, 181
  Red Velvet, 172, *173*
  Spice, with Lemon Sauce, *170*, 171
  Strawberry, Lizzie's, 158, *159*
  Strawberry Shortcake, Old-Fashioned, 164, *165*
California Pizza Kitchen, 73
candy, 206–13
  Chocolate, Crockpot, 206, *207*
  Divinity, Never-Fail, 212, *213*
  Peanut Butter Balls, "Miss" Mickey's, 208
  Peanut Butter Bars, 209
  Sweet and Saltines, *210*, 211
Candy Apples, Red, *56*, 57
capers, in Chicken Piccata, *100*, 101
Carrot Cake, *166*, 167–68
casseroles:
  Baked Bean, 133
  Broccoli, *118*, 119
  Cabbage, *130*, 131
  Chicken and Dressing, Linda's, 104
  Chicken and Wild Rice, *106*, 107
  Chicken Spinach Lasagne, 105
  Cowboy Lasagne, *92*, 93
  Potato, 132
  Spaghetti, Baked, *86*, 87
  Squash, 120, *121*
Cates, Colleen, 63
Catfish, Pete's, 109
Charleston Cheese Dip, *44*, 45

Cheddar cheese:
  Baked Spaghetti, *86*, 87
  Breakfast Bowl, Garth's, *24*, 25
  Broccoli Casserole, *118*, 119
  Cabbage Casserole, *130*, 131
  Charleston Cheese Dip, *44*, 45
  Cheese Boat, 48
  Chicken Pizza, 102, *103*
  Chicken Spinach Lasagne, 105
  Country Quiche, 26, 27
  Macaroni and Cheese, Crockpot, *122*, 123
  Potato Casserole, 132
  Squash Casserole, 120, *121*
  Stuffed Bell Peppers, Uncle Wilson's, *82*, 83
  Twice-Baked Potatoes, 128, *129*
  Vegetable Pie, 124, *125*
cheese:
  American, in Rainy Day Chicken and Rice Soup, 62
  Blue, Dressing, 66, 67
  Boat, 48
  Cowboy Lasagne, *92*, 93
  Dip, Charleston, *44*, 45
  grating your own vs. buying pre-shredded, 14
  Macaroni and, Crockpot, *122*, 123
  Monterey Jack, in Hot Corn Dip, 46
  pepper Jack, in Broccoli Cornbread, 150, *151*
  see also Cheddar cheese; cream cheese; mozzarella cheese; Parmesan cheese
cherry(ies):
  candied, in Fruitcake Cookies, 194, *195*
  Muffins, Miniature, Blanche's, 153
chicken, 99–107
  Bites, Warren's, 50, *50*
  and Dressing, Linda's, 104
  Piccata, *100*, 101
  Pizza, 102, *103*
  Poppy Seed Salad, 76, 77

  and Rice Soup, Rainy Day, 62
  Soup, *60*, 61
  Spinach Lasagne, 105
  and Wild Rice Casserole, *106*, 107
Chili, Fancy, 64, *65*
chocolate:
  Cake with Divinity Icing, *174*, 175–76
  Candy, Crockpot, 206, *207*
  Chip Cookies, Venita's, *191*, *196*, 197
  Peanut Butter Bars, 209
  Pie, 182–85, *183*
  Pinwheel Cookies, Lizzie's, *191*, 193
  Red Velvet Cake, 172, *173*
  Sweet and Saltines, *210*, 211
  Torte, 177–78, *179*
Cilantro-Lime Dressing, Sweet, *71*, 73
cinnamon:
  Rolls, 31, *35*
  sugar, making your own, 34
Clements, Lydia, *29*
Cliett, Dorothy, *212*
coconut:
  Apple Ambrosia, Betty's, *204*, 205
  Cake with Coconut Lemon Glaze, Grandma Yearwood's, 169
  Carrot Cake, *166*, 167–68
Cold-Oven Pound Cake, 163
Colleen's Cabbage Rolls, 84, *85*
Confectioners' Sugar Icing, 191
cookies, 189–99
  Chocolate Chip, Venita's, *191*, *196*, 197
  Chocolate Pinwheel, Lizzie's, *191*, 193
  Fruitcake, 194, *195*
  Iced Sugar, Jennifer's, 190–91, *191*
  Lemon Squares, *191*, 201
  Shortbread, Vicki's, 199
  Teacakes, Mamie's, *191*, 198
  Thumbprint, *191*, 192
Cordelia's Roast Beef, 88, *89*

corn:
    Dip, Hot, 46
    Low-Country Boil, 110, *111*
    Salsa, *40*, 41
cornbread:
    Broccoli, 150, *151*
    Chicken and Dressing, Linda's, 104
    Jalapeño Hushpuppies, 152
    Salad with French Dressing, *70*, 71
    Sour Cream, 144
corned beef, in Cheese Boat, 48
cottage cheese, in Shamrock Salad, 78
Country Quiche, 26, *27*
Cowboy Lasagne, *92*, 93
cranberry:
    Bread, *146*, 147
    Orange Relish, 134, *135*
cream cheese:
    Charleston Cheese Dip, *44*, 45
    Cheese Boat, 48
    Chicken Bites, Warren's, 50, *50*
    Frosting, *166*, 168, 172, *173*
    Grape Salad, 200, *200*
    Icing, 162
    Jalapeño Bites, 49
    Pumpkin Roll, *180*, 181
    Thumbprint Cookies, *191*, 192
crockpots, *see* slow cookers
Crunchy Slaw, 116, *117*
Crust, Graham Cracker, 182, 187
cucumbers, in Six-Week Pickles, *52*, 53

davis, Elizabeth, 150
Deraney, Lynn Newton, 194
desserts, 155–213
    Apple Ambrosia, Betty's, *204*, 205
    Chocolate Pie, 182–85, *183*
    Grape Salad, 200, *200*
    Lemon Meringue Pie, Magic, *186*, 187
    Peanut Butter Balls, "Miss" Mickey's, 208
    Pecan Tassies, Bess London's, 202, *203*
    Sweet Potato Pudding, *136*, 136–37

Whipped Cream, Homemade, 137
see also cakes; candy; cookies
dips:
    Cheese, Charleston, *44*, 45
    Corn, Hot, 46
    Corn Salsa, *40*, 41
    Edamame, Spicy, 47
    Watermelon Salsa, 42, *43*
divinity:
    Icing, *174*, 176
    Never-Fail, 212, *213*
doughnuts: Beignets, *36*, 37
Dressing, Chicken and, Linda's, 104
dressings (salad):
    Blue Cheese, *66*, 67
    French, 71
    Lime-Cilantro, Sweet, *71*, 73
    Sweet-and-Sour (for slaw), 116
Dumplings, Apple, 30, *31*

edamame:
    Dip, Spicy, 47
    Thai Salad, Ty's, *72*, 73
Edward's Pies, 187
eggs:
    Breakfast Bowl, Garth's, *24*, 25
    Country Quiche, 26, *27*
egg whites:
    Divinity Icing, *174*, 176
    Magic Lemon Meringue Pie, *186*, 187
    Meringue, 185
    Never-Fail Divinity, 212, *213*

fancy Chili, 64, *65*
fish and seafood, 99, 108–11
    Bass, Saucy, 108
    Catfish, Pete's, 109
    Low-Country Boil, 110, *111*
Foster, Pat Sizemore, 136
Fred's Barbecued Pork Ribs, *96*, 97
French Dressing, 71
frostings:
    Cream Cheese, *166*, 168, 172, *173*
    see also icings
Fruitcake Cookies, 194, *195*
Fruit Salad, Hawaiian, *28*, 29
Funderburke, Paula Lane, *185*

garth's Breakfast Bowl, *24*, 25
gelatin, in Shamrock Salad, 78
Georgia Pâté, 51
Gilliam, Emmett, 202
glazes:
    Buttermilk, *156*, 157
    Coconut Lemon, 169
Goodman, Cordelia, 88
graham cracker(s):
    Crust, 182, 187
    Sweet and Saltines, *210*, 211
Grandma Yearwood's Coconut Cake with Coconut Lemon Glaze, 169
grape(s):
    Chicken Poppy Seed Salad, 76, 77
    Salad, 200, *200*
green beans, in Marinated Vegetable Salad, 74

ham Salad, Uncle Marshall's, 75
Hash, Roast Beef, 88
Hawaiian Fresh Fruit Salad, *28*, 29
Helm, Pam, 208
Helm, Patty, 208
Herter, Jarrah, *13*
Hickey, Herb and Glenda, 116
Hot Corn Dip, 46
Hulsey, Sissy Tillman, 182, *185*
Hushpuppies, Jalapeño, 152

iced Sugar Cookies, Jennifer's, 190–91, *191*
icings:
    Confectioners' Sugar, 191
    Cream Cheese, 162
    Divinity, *174*, 176
    Strawberry, 158, *159*
    tools for, 15

jalapeño:
    Bites, 49
    Hushpuppies, 152
Jambalaya, Tennessee, 63
Jennifer's Iced Sugar Cookies, 190–91, *191*
Jordan, Mary Lou, 141

Key Lime Cake, *160*, 161–62
kielbasa, in Tennessee Jambalaya, 63
Kozma, Hope, 101

Lane, Sydney, *185*
lasagne:
    Chicken Spinach, 105
    Cowboy, *92*, 93
Leach, Peggy, 142
LeFlore, Kim, 91, 181
lemon:
    Coconut Glaze, 169
    Meringue Pie, Magic, *186*, 187
    Sauce, *170*, 171
    Squares, *191*, 201
Lettuce Wedge with Blue Cheese
        Dressing, *66*, 67
lime:
    Cilantro Dressing, Sweet, *71*, 73
    Key, Cake, *160*, 161–62
Linda's Chicken and Dressing, 104
Lizzie's Chocolate Pinwheel
        Cookies, *191*, 193
Lizzie's Strawberry Cake, 158, *159*
London, Bess, 202
Low-Country Boil, 110, *111*

Macaroni and Cheese, Crock-
        pot, *122*, 123
Magic Lemon Meringue Pie, *186*,
        187
Mama's Homemade Waffles with
        Hot Maple Syrup, *18*, 19–20,
        21
Mamie's Teacakes, *191*, 198
Maple Syrup, Hot, 20, *21*
Margaret's Raisin Bread, 145
Marinated Vegetable Salad, 74
marshmallows, in Divinity Icing, *174*,
        176
Martin, Sara, 194
Martin, Vicki, 48
Maxwell, Betty, 171, 205
McCormack, Mandy, 88, 148
McCormack, Pat, 148
Meatballs, 91
Meringue, 185
    Pie, Lemon, Magic, *186*, 187

meringue powder, 191
Miniature Cherry Muffins,
        Blanche's, 153
"Miss" Mickey's Peanut Butter Balls,
        208
Monkey Bread, *33*
    Muffins, *32*, 33
Monterey Jack cheese:
    Charleston Cheese Dip, *44*, 45
    Hot Corn Dip, 46
Monticello Woman's Club, 200
mozzarella cheese:
    Baked Spaghetti, *86*, 87
    Chicken Pizza, 102, *103*
    Cowboy Lasagne, *92*, 93
    Vegetable Pie, *124*, *125*
muffins:
    Cherry, Miniature, Blanche's, 153
    Easiest, *140*, 141
    Monkey Bread, *32*, 33
Murrelle, Mary, 198
mushrooms:
    Chicken and Wild Rice Casserole,
        106, 107
    Chicken Spinach Lasagne, 105

Napa cabbage, in Ty's Thai Salad,
        72, 73
Never-Fail Divinity, 212, *213*
Newton, Fannie, 194
Nichols, Charlie, 133
noodles, *see* pasta; ramen noodles

Oat(meal):
    Chocolate Chip Cookies, Venita's,
        191, *196*, 197
    Peanut Butter Bars, 209
offset spatulas, 15
Okra and Tomatoes, *114*, 115
Old-Fashioned Strawberry Short-
        cake, 164, *165*
orange:
    Apple Ambrosia, Betty's, *204*, 205
    Cranberry Relish, 134, *135*
    Pork Medallions, 94, *95*
Ozburn, Bobbie Jean, 200

Pancakes, Blueberry, 22, *23*
Parmesan cheese:
    Cowboy Lasagne, *92*, 93
    Hot Corn Dip, 46
    Jalapeño Bites, 49
    Strawberry Salad, 68, *69*
pasta:
    Baked Spaghetti, *86*, 87
    Chicken Soup, *60*, 61
    Chicken Spinach Lasagne, 105
    Cowboy Lasagne, *92*, 93
    Crockpot Macaroni and Cheese,
        122, 123
    tortellini, in Garth's Breakfast
        Bowl, *24*, 25
Pâté, Georgia, 51
Pat's Pumpkin Bread, 148
Paulk, Beth, 83
Paulk, Cora, 76
Paulk, Donna, 61, 206
Paulk, Elizabeth "Lizzie," 107, 158,
        164, 175, 193
Paulk, Fred, 97
Paulk, Grandaddy, 108, 175
Paulk, Linda, 104
Paulk, Marshall Edwards, 75, *75*
Paulk, Mary, 108
Paulk, Warren, 50
Paulk, Wilson, 83
Paulk, Winnes, 175
peanut(s):
    Butter Balls, "Miss" Mickey's, 208
    Butter Bars, 209
    Crockpot Chocolate Candy, 206,
        207
    Georgia Pâté, 51
peas, in Marinated Vegetable Salad, 74
pecan(s):
    Fruitcake Cookies, 194, *195*
    Grape Salad, 200, *200*
    Monkey Bread Muffins, *32*, 33
    Never-Fail Divinity, 212, *213*
    Pumpkin Roll, *180*, 181
    Tassies, Bess London's, 202, *203*
    Thumbprint Cookies, *191*, 192
pepper Jack cheese, in Broccoli
        Cornbread, 150, *151*
Peppers, Stuffed Bell, Uncle
        Wilson's, *82*, 83

Perry, Edwin, 119
Perry, Julianne, 119
Perry, Julie, 119
Perry, Melissa, 147
Pete's Catfish, 109
Pickles, Six-Week, *52*, 53
pie plates, disposable metal, 15
pies (savory):
    Country Quiche, 26, *27*
    Vegetable, 124, *125*
pies (sweet), 155, 182–87
    Chocolate, 182–85, *183*
    Graham Cracker Crust for, 182,
        187
    Lemon Meringue, Magic, *186*,
        187
pineapple:
    Apple Ambrosia, Betty's, *204*,
        205
    candied, in Fruitcake Cookies,
        194, *195*
    Carrot Cake, *166*, 167–68
    Shamrock Salad, 78
Pinwheel Cookies, Chocolate,
    Lizzie's, *191*, 193
Pizza, Chicken, 102, *103*
Poppy Seed Chicken Salad, 76, 77
pork, 81, 90–97
    Ham Salad, Uncle Marshall's, 75
    Loin, Slow-Cooker, 90
    Meatballs, 91
    Medallions, 94, *95*
    Ribs, Barbecued, Fred's, *96*, 97
    see also bacon; sausage
potato(es):
    Breakfast Bowl, Garth's, *24*, 25
    Casserole, 132
    Low-Country Boil, 110, *111*
    Twice-Baked, 128, *129*
Pound Cake, Cold-Oven, 163
Pritchett, Phyllis, 42
Pudding, Sweet Potato, *136*,
    136–37
pumpkin:
    Bread, Pat's, 148
    Roll, *180*, 181

quiche, Country, 26, *27*

rainy Day Chicken and Rice Soup,
    62
raisin(s):
    Bread, Margaret's, 145
    Fruitcake Cookies, 194, *195*
ramen noodles:
    Crunchy Slaw, 116, *117*
    Strawberry Salad, 68, *69*
red cabbage, in Ty's Thai Salad, 72,
    73
Red Candy Apples, *56*, 57
Red Velvet Cake, 172, *173*
Relish, Cranberry-Orange, 134, *135*
Ribs, Barbecued Pork, Fred's, *96*,
    97
rice:
    Cabbage Rolls, Colleen's, 84, *85*
    and Chicken Soup, Rainy Day,
        62
    Stuffed Bell Peppers, Uncle
        Wilson's, *82*, 83
Rice Krispie's, in "Miss" Mickey's
    Peanut Butter Balls, 208
Richey, Amanda Akins, 209
ricotta cheese, in Cowboy Lasagne,
    92, 93
rolls:
    Cinnamon, 34, *35*
    Spoon, 142, *143*
romaine lettuce:
    Cornbread Salad with French
        Dressing, 70, 71
    Strawberry Salad, 68, *69*
Rundorff, Lindsey, 76

Salads, 59, 67–79
    Apple Ambrosia, Betty's, *204*, 205
    Chicken Poppy Seed, 76, 77
    Cornbread, with French Dressing,
        70, 71
    Fresh Fruit, Hawaiian, *28*, 29
    Grape, 200, *200*
    Ham, Uncle Marshall's, 75
    Lettuce Wedge with Blue Cheese
        Dressing, *66*, 67
    Marinated Vegetable, 74
    Shamrock, 78
    Slaw, Crunchy, 116, *117*
    Strawberry, 68, *69*

    Thai, Ty's, *72*, 73
    see also dressings
salsas:
    Corn, *40*, 41
    Watermelon, 42, *43*
saltine crackers, in Sweet and Sal-
    tines, *210*, 211
Sandifer, Venita, 197
sauces:
    Lemon, *170*, 171
    see also dressings
Saucy Bass, 108
sausage:
    Breakfast Bowl, Garth's, *24*, 25
    Country Quiche, 26, *27*
    Cowboy Lasagne, *92*, 93
    kielbasa, in Tennessee Jambalaya,
        63
    Low-Country Boil, 110, *111*
seafood, *see* fish and seafood
Sealy, Gail, 172
Shamrock Salad, 78
Shortbread, Vicki's, 199
Shortcake, Strawberry, Old-
    Fashioned, 164, *165*
Shoup, Gail, 133, 177
shrimp, in Low-Country Boil, 110,
    111
sides, 113–37
    Asparagus Bundles, *126*, 127
    Baked Bean Casserole, 133
    Broccoli Casserole, *118*, 119
    Cabbage Casserole, *130*, 131
    Cranberry-Orange Relish, 134,
        135
    Macaroni and Cheese, Crockpot,
        122, 123
    Okra and Tomatoes, *114*, 115
    Potato Casserole, 132
    Potatoes, Twice-Baked, 128, *129*
    Slaw, Crunchy, 116, *117*
    Squash Casserole, 120, *121*
    Sweet Potato Pudding, *136*,
        136–37
    Vegetable Pie, 124, *125*
    see also breads
Six-Week Pickles, *52*, 53
Sizemore, Ora, 136
Slaw, Crunchy, 116, *117*
slow cookers (crockpots), 14

Chocolate Candy, Crockpot, 206, 207
Macaroni and Cheese, 122, 123
Pork Loin, 90
snacks and appetizers, 39–57
Cheese Boat, 48
Cheese Dip, Charleston, 44, 45
Chicken Bites, Warren's, 50, 50
Corn Dip, Hot, 46
Corn Salsa, 40, 41
Edamame Dip, Spicy, 47
Georgia Pâté, 51
Jalapeño Bites, 49
Meatballs, 91
Pickles, Six-Week, 52, 53
Red Candy Apples, 56, 57
Sweet Tea, 54, 55
Watermelon Salsa, 42, 43
soups, 59–62
Chicken, 60, 61
Chicken and Rice, Rainy Day, 62
see also stews
Sour Cream Cornbread, 144
Spaghetti, Baked, 86, 87
spatulas, offset, 15
Spice Cake with Lemon Sauce, 170, 171
Spicy Edamame Dip, 47
spinach:
Chicken Lasagne, 105
Strawberry Salad, 68, 69
Spivey, Angela, 12
Spoon Rolls, 142, 143
squash (summer):
Casserole, 120, 121
Vegetable Pie, 124, 125
Yellow, Cornbread, 150, 151
Zucchini Bread, 149
Stamper, Howard and Mickey, 208
stand mixers, Beater Blade for, 15
stews:
Chili, Fancy, 64, 65
Jambalaya, Tennessee, 63
strawberry:
Cake, Lizzie's, 158, 159
Salad, 68, 69
Shortcake, Old-Fashioned, 164, 165
Stuffed Bell Peppers, Uncle Wilson's, 82, 83

sugar:
cinnamon, making your own, 34
Confectioners', Icing, 191
Cookies, Iced, Jennifer's, 190–91, 191
sunflower seeds, in Strawberry Salad, 68, 69
Sweet and Saltines, 210, 211
Sweet Lime-Cilantro Dressing, 71, 73
Sweet Potato Pudding, 136, 136–37
Sweet Tea, 54, 55

Tahini, in Georgia Pâté, 51
Tea, Sweet, 54, 55
Teacakes, Mamie's, 191, 198
Tennessee Jambalaya, 63
Thai Salad, Ty's, 72, 73
Thumbprint Cookies, 191, 192
Tillman, Bill, 182, 185
Tillman, Mack, 182
Tomatoes, Okra and, 114, 115
Torte, Chocolate, 177–78, 179
tortellini, in Garth's Breakfast Bowl, 24, 25
turkey, ground, in Fancy Chili, 64, 65
turntables, cake-decorating, 15
Twice-Baked Potatoes, 128, 129
Ty's Thai Salad, 72, 73

Uncle Marshall's Ham Salad, 75
Uncle Wilson's Stuffed Bell Peppers, 82, 83

Vanilla wafers, in Grandma Yearwood's Coconut Cake with Coconut Lemon Glaze, 169
vegetable(s):
Pie, 124, 125
Salad, Marinated, 74
see also sides
Venita's Chocolate Chip Cookies, 191, 196, 197
Vicki's Shortbread, 199
Vincent, Jennifer, 190, 192
Vining, Chrystal, 75

Waffles:
bacon, 20
Mama's Homemade, with Hot Maple Syrup, 18, 19–20, 21
Walker, Vicki, 34, 134, 199
walnuts:
Carrot Cake, 166, 167–68
Fresh Apple Cakae, 156, 157
Never-Fail Divinity, 212, 213
Warren's Chicken Bites, 50, 50
Watermelon Salsa, 42, 43
Watson, Margaret, 145
Weber, Tana, 167
Whipped Cream, Homemade, 137
Wild Rice and Chicken Casserole, 106, 107
Wilson, Nona, 53
Wilton Cake Release, 15, 178
Workman, Stone, 101

Yearwood, Bo, 78
Yearwood, Elizabeth Winslett, 78, 169
Yearwood, Gwen, 19, 29, 34, 37, 49, 50, 51, 53, 57, 74, 78, 83, 107, 108, 109, 119, 134, 137, 141, 142, 145, 161, 169, 172, 175, 187, 209, 211, 212
Yearwood, Jack, 34, 47, 50, 78, 109, 116, 161, 169, 194, 205
Yearwood, Pete, 109
Yearwood, SuSan, 19
yellow squash:
Cornbread, 150, 151
Squash Casserole, 120, 121
Vegetable Pie, 124, 125

Zucchini:
Bread, 149
Vegetable Pie, 124, 125